EVERY DAY, I DO

HOW TO REWRITE YOUR VOWS AFTER AN AFFAIR

ANGEL MYERS

Copyright 2023 Angel Myers LMFT

No part of this book may be produced or used in any manner without the author's and copyright owner's written consent.

All Rights Reserved

AMF Publishing

Contact: info@marriageandfamily.com

Angel Marriage & Family Services
Help when it matters the most...

Disclaimer: The characters in this book are a work of fiction. Any resemblances to persons living or dead purely coincidental. Furthermore, this book does not replace the advice of a medical or behavioral health professional guidance. Consult your medical or behavioral health provider before making any clinical decisions pertaining to your mental health or medical care. This book covers content which some may find triggering. Therefore, proceed as desired and discontinue if you find any material which causes discomfort. Any referenced material in this book was correct at the time of publication, but the Author does not assume liability for loss or damage caused by errors or omissions.

Contents

Introduction 4
The Discovery 6

01. A Journey to Healing the Relationship: A Case Example 12
02. Navigating Panic and Fear 24
03. "Is This Normal?" 36
04. Marriage Bonding 44
05. Communication 51
06. Empathy 62
07. Intimacy 66
08. Trust 72
09. Emotional Regulation: How to Manage Your Triggers 80
10. When to Seek Professional Help 89
11. Rewriting Your Vows 99

Appendix 103
Notes 104
About the Author 107

Every Day, I Do: Journaling Through Betrayal 108
Introduction 110
Self Nurturance: 112
Private Wins 121
Dreams 130
How Do I Feel 139
Stay in Faith 148
Time Capsule To My Younger Self 157
Appendix 159

INTRODUCTION

Expectations for This Book

In this book, you will find a blueprint for incorporating your own closely held beliefs and plans into a process of recovering from the affair in your marriage. This is not a rigid blueprint for repairing your marriage, but rather a plan that can be customized to fit your specific needs as you move through the healing journey.

At the end of each chapter, you will find a section for taking notes as well as a writing prompt for additional reflection.

The contents of each chapter are designed to highlight important components of your relationship blueprint. The chapters are not ordered in any hierarchical order; instead, they are positioned for access at any point in your relationship journey. They represent typically addressed topics during the process of affair recovery and are designed to fully address as many key elements as possible to help you move toward a return to a healthy marriage.

Lastly, you and your partner will establish a new charge in the restoration of your relationship, just as you did on your wedding day. You will recommit and, for some, rewrite your wedding vows in order to record and mark the new calibrations of your marriage. This will be an opportunity to gather and collect the lessons learned in this process and also to reestablish the required tasks necessary to reflect the marriage vows in a systematic way every day.

As you and your spouse identify ways in which you will each accept the position benefits of partners as well as the daily responsibilities, you will find this book a resource to help provide information, practical tools, and encouragement along the way.

In conclusion, the hope for this book is that you and your partner will become more familiar with the landscape of affair recovery. This book may be viewed as an orientation to the journey of repairing your marriage. It may also be a resource to help you determine what tools you will want and find most valuable for the process of healing your relationship. While this book is not meant to provide advice for the initial decision to repair the relationship, it can be a reference point for understanding what may be helpful once that decision has been made.

THE DISCOVERY

How do you reconcile truth with the truth?

The truth is that you still love your partner. You are committed and have been from the beginning. Equally true is the devastation you feel about staying together.

It is confusing to think back on how yesterday the vows to love, honor, and cherish had seemingly always operated in the background. Now the fragility of those vows is at the forefront of your mind; they seem much less permanent. When they were in the background, the vows formed a foundation upon which everything was built. There was no need to revisit them—or so it seemed. Like a fixture, those vows were lasting improvements to a developing relationship structure.

You have asked "What is true?" before, but now, everything is up for questioning. It's more than the marriage and more than the family you created. The question shows up in your friendships, in your business, in the life you've always known, and now in you. The question penetrates every layer of your world, and the answer is elusive in every dimension.

The truth is that on the day "I do" was pledged, the officiant looked at new love, new forever, new hope, new future, and affirmed before others that this relationship, recorded before history, would now and forever be known as an unbreakable bond between you two.

The truth is that the truth does not seem as true as it once did. The truth seems to be evolving. The truth looks different now. It's hardly recognizable—so much so that your question changes: Is truth even truth? You contemplate whether it was just a lie after all.

The paradox is that the more you learn, the less you know.

You find yourself searching for any clue. You look online for digital footprints. You check receipts. You check accounts, records, bills, friends, and/or family. The act of checking is exhausting. You find yourself looking for any clue now that you know, even though every clue leads to another. It eventually becomes a cycle where you may feel compelled to look, to know. You don't want to know, but you must know.

Sometimes you wonder whether it is compulsion or just part of the process of getting everything out on the table before proceeding with the next steps in your marriage. It is the searching and checking that have led to seeking some sort of relief.

You ask yourself, *How do I get past these feelings? How do I forgive? How do I move on?*

You've already decided that you want to stay for now, but the conflict causes you to waver. You know you both need help, but you are unsure where to begin.

By now, you have concluded that there has been infidelity in your marriage. If you are wondering whether others have endured the trials and pains of an affair, know that you and your partner are not alone.

More than the anecdotal stories or made-for-television dramas that depict the stages of healing in less than thirty minutes, including commercials, infidelity is a dynamic challenge that many couples face. It is dynamic in the sense that the introduction of an unwanted party in the relational dyad can affect the relationship in a myriad of ways.

In television shows, there is a feature of intrigue and scandal where a couple entrenched in the controversy process the affair in rudimentary and simplistic ways. These relationships are often featured and discussed in ways that highlight reconciliation and forgiveness with minimal study on the profound impact on the individual and the marriage. In reality, one of the most important parts of the story is where the couple begins the arduous process toward recovery.

In these stories, in some ways, it seems as though the recovery process is romanticized. In this process, there is a moment of discovery, then grief, a simple strategy, and voilà! The marriage is better than ever. Sure, there is pain in the process, but in the end, everything is fine. In fact, it's as if nothing ever happened. But the real story is much more complex.

The fallacy of this depiction is that most times, couples will never forget the period of the marriage in which the affair marked a clear shift in their relationship.

The issue is not that there is an inability to move on from the pain of the affair, forgive, and engage more healthily in the relationship. The challenge is that the memory of working your way back to one another is something very few ever forget. It is as if you have discovered that your marriage was recently inflicted with a very serious illness, one which, without the proper medicine, could lead to a series of potentially fatal consequences.

Your marriage is not a person, of course, but imagine for a moment that your marriage had its own identity, determination, and inherent interests, just as if it were a person. If you were a person diagnosed with a life-changing illness, your first response might be to research and study information about the condition and its typical course. Then you might find yourself reading and seeking any literature pertaining to treatments, effectiveness, and, lastly, prognosis. Much of this material will either give you hope or heap layers of additional emotional weight on top of the fear and confusion you may already be carrying. You will seek out the best doctor and medical provider for your recommended care, and you will begin the worthy fight of life. Your marriage is this person.

Yes, your marriage is not a real person, nor is your marriage a television show or the collective anecdotes passed from one generation to another. Instead, your marriage can be viewed as separate from you and your partner.

In this perspective, the marriage is its own entity, and you and your partner are the substance of which it is made. Viewing it from this angle can help partners orient themselves to the objective of treatment in affair recovery. If you are unsure of what that is, let's be clear here.

The objective is to identify the illness, injury, or affliction that has occurred in the marriage in order to evaluate and ascertain the most appropriate and effective course of treatment, knowing that there are no guarantees. The process is dynamic and different for every couple, which makes the prescribed intervention or strength unique for each relationship. But with steady, consistent care, the hope is that, in the end, not only will the marriage have survived the initial injury, but the course of treatment will have helped to heal the underlying cause(s) that may have existed.

While you may feel alone, you are not alone. There are a number of individuals who will encounter a relational affair during their lifetime. According to researchers John and Julie Gottman, authors of the course *Treating Affairs and Trauma*, "USA rates in convenience samples vary from 15 to 43% of men and 10 to 15% of women being sexually unfaithful throughout their marriages."[1] Understanding this prevalence helps to remove the isolation and loneliness. As a member of this group, you may find yourself shrunken and yet filled with a multitude of emotions. Some feelings that are unique to loneliness include shame, guilt, and embarrassment. Here you tell yourself that you only have you.

The reality is that you are in the company of many other people in monogamous relationships that either have dealt or will deal with marital infidelity. There is no comfort in the company of turmoil, but there may be comfort in knowing that, like others who have experienced infidelity within their marriage, you too can journey through a well-worn path directing you toward clearer steps. There is a way forward.

Vows and Expectations

The average couple does not reference their vows during their day-to-day life. Instead, it is during moments of celebration or distress when the marriage will more often undergo review or scrutiny, depending on the motivating circumstances.

Similarly, in times of crisis, where one may pray and meditate using sacraments of their faith, so it is with couples that in moments of distress the vows and promises of marriage are called into question. This crisis of belief cracks the foundation of one's perception of self and others. It calls into question what you expected and things that you knew for sure. Suddenly everything you expected now looks uncertain and unsure.

Expectations are like assurances. It is *when you know that you know*. It is the place where doubts are canceled. This is often what happens when we enter into marriage. There's a surety in the relationship. It even feels different. It is not like a couple getting to know one another and beginning the dance of pursuit and permission. Instead, it is where two decide, after enough dancing, to let the music play. There is no last song in space.

We depend on these expectations of the relationship as part of our day-to-day normality. However, when there has been a tear in the fabric of the relationship, the rip can be felt in all the layers. What you expected and what you know for sure are no longer clear. In fact, it is the proverbial ripping and tearing through your intrapsychic expectations that quake the bedrock of your soul deep within. Within the cracks lie the broken expectations, the broken promises, and shaken assurances. This can add to a profound feeling of loss. Shattered expectations are like a window that was once well-paned, behind whose glass emotional safety and vulnerability once resided; that window is now fragmented, and what remains is scattered. This emotional fragmentation can feel sudden when you find out that your partner has been unfaithful.

History of the Wedding Vows

"I do" are two words that often begin a marriage. Though brief in expression, the meaning of these words has the capacity to take a relationship from among a sea of many to a paramount place in one's life and the lives of those surrounding it. The power of these words has the capacity to create and multiply its product, the individual. In the beginning, there is one—and then there are two.

"I do" begins with a promise to bond two lives in love and commitment. This promise seems infallible. It's the truth upon which you built an entire life. This promise helped craft your plans, your hopes, and your dreams. In fact, it's so powerful that from it life often springs anew. The promise began with two, and then there were more. Now, after the affair, this fruitful display of relationship synergy becomes threatened by disconnection and therefore risks the combined health of the individuals in the marriage entity.

Traditional wedding vows have been present for centuries. Many sacred rituals signify the passage from one station to another. They are a guidepost for the nature of the relationship that composes the terms.

These terms may include more commonly used expressions we frequently hear at many nuptials: *To have and to hold, from this day forward, for richer and for poorer*, and *'til death do us part* are just a few. This portion of the ceremony may even include personally written vows that reflect a couple's unique promises. Rarely is a ceremony missing this heritage, this long-held custom in which two declare their promises before others. These promises form the foundation on which this newly solidified relationship will exist. Before witnesses, this step in the ceremony has often come to be known as the pinnacle of the wedding ritual. The vows become a beacon shining a light on the expectations of the relationship. These expectations give way to canonized collections of commitments recorded in history and for all eternity.

CHAPTER 1

A JOURNEY TO HEALING THE RELATIONSHIP: A CASE EXAMPLE

In this book, we will follow a fictitious couple through a journey from a budding marriage to the near demise of their marriage due to infidelity. The purpose of this fictitious couple is to serve as an example of stages a couple may transition through and, most importantly, as hope for the possible tools you may use to also find relief and eventual resolve from the most pressing effects on your relationship of the aftermath of an affair. This couple should only be of service to you as you contemplate how components of the book and the couple's story will apply to you; this book is not meant to specifically diagnose and/or treat your specific circumstances. It is instead my fervent desire that this book will shine a light on the possibilities that exist in your pursuit to recover and heal your marriage.

Rebecca and Kevin

Rebecca and Kevin had been married for eight years. They had four children, all of whom were from previous relationships. Rebecca had been single for several years before meeting Kevin.

She was a single parent to two children and had never been married. Raising two children as a single parent came with its own challenges; however, she was accustomed to doing things on her own. She was proud of the family life she was creating and was not looking for a new relationship. Instead, she was interested in building her career, raising her children, and building a life she could be proud of. Then someone entered her life. After several years as a single mom, she met someone at a work engagement. His name was Kevin. He was a recently divorced father of two. He was in the same industry as Rebecca, and they had mutual friendships. The connection was immediate, and after a brief period of casual dating, they soon agreed to a committed relationship. Kevin was looking for a wife, as he enjoyed being married. Though his first marriage had ended in divorce, he looked forward to remarrying.

Eventually, Rebecca and Kevin became engaged, even though Rebecca had not been looking for marriage. She knew that if she were ever to find someone she wanted to marry, that it would be for the rest of her life. She knew that in marrying someone there would be challenges, but she was determined that any future relationship would be different from the conflict-riddled relationships she had been accustomed to seeing during her childhood. Her marriage would be based on honesty, communication, and fidelity. She believed she had found that in Kevin. In fact, it seemed easy with him, even though she had not had a lot of experience in long-term romantic love. Her previous relationship, which had led to having her two children, had spanned a couple of years, though it had been intermittent. She told herself that her new relationship was constant, stable, and secure. She thought her connection with Kevin was the recipe for a long, happy relationship.

Kevin, on the other hand, knew relationships required work. It had been hard for him to heal from the previous failed marriage. He had loved his ex-wife but had often found it hard to resolve conflicts within their relationship. Kevin had often felt misunderstood and isolated within the relationship. His wife at the time had had her own concerns as well. As hard as they had tried to resolve conflict, it had always ended with more misunderstanding, miscommunication, and increasing feelings of loneliness. Eventually, the relationship ended in divorce, and Kevin knew that if he ever remarried, it would be with someone who understood him. It would be with someone who could communicate with him. Instead of isolation, he would have a partner who could stand by his side. It seemed to Kevin that he had found all of those things in Rebecca. The only thing left to do was to make it official by proposing and eventually marrying.

Life as a married couple initially was fun and exciting. The children—all four from previous relationships—had begun to adjust to living in a blended family. All the things Kevin and Rebecca had hoped for in a relationship were theirs for the taking. Happy and satisfied with how things were moving along, both enjoyed all the benefits of having a partner by their side. Communication about the relationship happened frequently early on. The space for intimacy happened naturally. There was no need for date night, because the romance and passion were effortless. Family time was happening regularly. It was a by-product of all the busyness that originated from the marriage and the couple's ease at enjoying time with each other and as a family. Life with each other was perfect. Life with each other was automatic. It wasn't hard; it also wasn't easy, but the formula seemed simple: keep things as they are, and they will always be that way.

Kevin and Rebecca came to see me when they questioned whether their marriage could survive its latest challenge. They were at a point in the relationship where they were determining whether they should continue in the marriage. They had been married for eight years by that point, and during the seventh year, Rebecca cheated on Kevin. Though hurt, Kevin decided that he was going to work on forgiving Rebecca and that the two would work on their marriage. Rebecca felt tremendous guilt for having caused Kevin pain and was anxious to repair the relationship. Both were concerned about what impact their relationship distress would have on the children and wanted to begin counseling as soon as possible.

During their first session, Rebecca began sharing what brought them both to counseling. She shared as if she were reciting a confession. As if a dam were being released, a burst of emotion poured from Rebecca as she explained with explicit personal accountability how she was the cause of their marriage being on the brink of divorce. She shared how much she loved her partner and that she was still confused about how she had allowed what started off as friendly dialogue with a coworker to lead to moments of betrayal in her marriage; she felt as though she had betrayed herself.

During the session, Kevin listened. He listened and motioned toward his partner during the parts of the story when she became emotional. He listened, although he vacillated at times. It was as if he was hearing an orchestra wading into the low notes even as he anticipated the crescendo. Kevin went between moments of physically comforting his partner and periods of sharp accusations concerning his partner's motives for infidelity. He too was confused by the internal conflict of loving his wife, wanting to care for her in distress, and his acute feelings of anger and sadness when reminded of what felt like another impending failure in marriage. Almost indistinguishable was this feeling of failure, both within the marriage and within himself.

Kevin and Rebecca recounted their relationship history during the intake. I had asked each of them when they had first determined there were problems within the marriage. Though they had initiated the session for Rebecca's infidelity, it was clear that this issue was just one example of the challenges that had begun long before the cheating. Much of what they described during the session included periods of distress within the marriage. Rifts in the marriage were expressed as points in a timeline where each partner lent a detail to explain their perspective of the range of conflicts more fully. Though the stories were from a shared history, both reported hearing parts of the story they had never heard before. I asked them what daily rituals they had implemented to reconcile problems within the marriage. And though they each could share examples of how they had discussed problems, there was no clear pathway they used to journey back to reconciliation. Since there was no clear plan and no rituals for healing, resolving, or bonding, challenges were addressed in the moment or many times not at all. Every day brought its own unique challenges. There was no need to address every conflict or moment of distress; the important things required attention, but the small conflicts were to be expected.

Over time, however, the small things weren't so small, such as the moments when Rebecca wanted to share her annoyance about the lights being turned on while she was still asleep and her partner was waking up for work. It wasn't that she did not understand her partner's need for light in the early dawn of the day as he prepared for work. The issue was how insensitive it seemed in the way he woke up and jostled about, making noise and turning on every switch to form a festival of lights that began in the bedroom. This was a simple thing, she told herself. *After all, aren't annoyances to be expected?* she would often ask herself. Though she had made her concerns known about the lights being turned on when she was resting in preparation for her workday, there was no need to revisit the issue. She told herself that marriage was about compromise and sometimes overlooking things. If her husband was insensitive in this area, then surely he made up for it tenfold in other ways.

Kevin held a very similar perspective. He had noticed his wife tended to change the subject when a conversation developed into an argument. It wasn't that the arguments ever escalated to yelling, screaming, name-calling, or the like; it was how the topic of conversation would switch abruptly to a new topic of discussion. Kevin eventually mentioned to Rebecca that doing so was rude and inhibited him from sharing his true thoughts. It didn't happen all the time, but when it did, it reminded Kevin of how selfish it seemed when his partner would cease to speak about an issue when the conversation did not go her way. When these moments occurred, Kevin was reminded of his previous marriage, where feelings of disconnection and being alone had been all too familiar. Rebecca did modify her actions to some degree, but Kevin still questioned whether they could discuss an issue without Rebecca shutting down. Did she truly hear him? And when that question came up inside of Kevin, the answer usually came as a resounding "no." After a while, it became more of an issue to address the issue than to pretend it wasn't even an issue at all.

Until eventually every issue was an issue. There were no small challenges. Everything seemed big. Conflicts felt overwhelming even before a word was said. So many times, nothing was said. Sure, sometimes things would rise to the surface. Like a pressure cooker, there were moments between the couple where they would argue or state concerns to each other. However, the feelings, the thoughts, and the ways in which they sought to protect themselves from what had become cyclical disappointment were rarely—if ever—addressed. Instead of addressing the pain of disappointment, they resigned themselves to acceptance. This was the way things would be. While in this space, there was a sense of helplessness. Oddly enough, there was also a perceived level of safety in no longer hoping for the hopeless and risking feelings of disappointment again. This was the marriage every day.

Every Day, I Do

Marriage is every day. The assumption is that after the vows, a demonstration of the relationship in its most complete form begins. Yes, there may be challenges that arise through the span of the relationship. However, everything that is needed is in the union—at least this is how it is often seen.

We often hear ubiquitous phrases for how we ought to approach marriage. Sometimes there are shreds of truth in these commonly shared quotes. Take, for instance, the phrase *marriage is work*. What does it mean? That marriage is a job? Marriage requires effort? If marriage requires work, what type of work? If marriage were a job, how often would you show up to work?

What are the position requirements? What are the hours? What is the payment exchange, and are there any benefits? What do performance evaluations look like, and how often would evaluations be conducted? If marriage is work, how frequently are we attending to the duties and obligations that we hold in position? Ask yourself, *if my marriage was a job, would my daily tasks of married life be different? Would my tasks today reflect that of one performing the duties of a healthy marriage?*

The importance of asking yourself these questions determine whether your efforts in marriage, the commitment to marriage, and the interventions are just as important as the application to marriage.

Marriage is like a job: it requires work. An employer anticipates the level of training and expertise that you bring in filling the position. The same will be true in what knowledge, skills, and regular application of those elements you bring in fulfilling the duties of your role as a partner, the duties to which you agreed on your wedding day when you spoke your vows. Therefore, marriage is a daily application of your vows. Your personal selection of strategies and philosophies of relationships are the ways in which you regularly implement your vows.

For instance, imagine having captured your dream job. Maybe you are already working in your dream job. Think back to the excitement you had anticipating your first day of work and all that you had envisioned. Having this dream position offers the possibility to change the trajectory of your future and help accomplish the life goals you've set for yourself. Performing the tasks each day at work becomes a noble gesture to get closer to your plans.

Now imagine the day you knew your partner was the one for you. Think back to the visions you had for your future. The opportunity for life together seemed limitless. The excitement of beginning a new life together was matched only by the day you actually shared your vows. This was the day you confirmed the position you hold for one another. The promise of forever had no expiration. This was the role of a lifetime.

Both examples highlight the aspirations of agreement in fidelity to a common goal. The difference is that in the marriage scenario, rarely do we take our wedding vows to explicitly mean an agreement to perform daily duties that regularly reflect the promises, vows, and goals that we also endeavor toward in marriage. Nonetheless, much like a job, when we accepted the offer to regularly deliver services in exchange for all the perks that came with having the job, we find ourselves also requiring the same daily attendance and regularity in providing deliverables within the marriage.

In essence, the words *I do*, those words recorded during the wedding day, signified one's formal job acceptance or—better said—your formal acceptance of the position of husband or wife in order to strategically carry out daily assignments in managing the overall tasks for the marriage entity.

If only Rebecca and Kevin had known that many times small issues were seeds for larger issues left unmanaged. Though seemingly insignificant, now Kevin's propensity for waking her up in the morning was just another example of his insensitivity to her needs. Now so deeply rooted are the small issues that they are easily overlooked. They cause no initial concern that leads either spouse to change the ways in which the rest of the relationship is tended to. In fact, you may not fully even be cognizant of the presence of these smaller issues.

Perhaps you have identified the seeds of these new types of issues in the field of your marriage and are able to see that some conflicts or feelings of discomfort occasionally sprout from the small seedlings. However, you calculate that it is manageable and not likely to ruin the rest of the cultivation. Gradually things change, but the change is not enough in the beginning to activate a full response to the slow invasion of the weeds that crop up. Instead, it is eventual, steady, and stealthy. Because of the nature by which the undesired small issues arise, you become accustomed to the new growth. You begin to make room for the new yield. After a while, the beginnings suddenly become full-grown. What you and your partner were planting has now been infiltrated by so many other issues that it can feel overwhelming—you don't know where to begin the process of addressing what stays and what goes. You find yourselves in full response to what now feels like an impending demise of all that you worked and hoped for, and depending on your response to an emotional threat, you may take on myriads of coping mechanisms.

For instance, in response to what feels like a multitude of issues in your relationship—or the insurmountable feeling of being unable to overcome these issues—you may attempt to address your partner in communication or you may seek counsel outside of your marriage with a local church, friends, or family. In this space of worry, you look for anything that might help your relationship because you have a sense of urgency.

Maybe you are more the type to turn inward to address the growing challenges in your marriage. On the outside, you may seem uncaring or nonchalant, but inside, you are waging a full battle against the spread of immense negativity and the fading dream of your beautiful relationship garden. Here, you wonder if everything is ruined and if there is anything left. You hope there is.

Kevin and Rebecca began the intentional journey back to one another, or rather they began the journey back to themselves. The couple learned in the process of doing work to repair their marriage that they each had unmet emotional needs, things they longed for in their marriage. In fact, having a glimpse and perhaps even moments of met emotional needs early on in their relationship likely bonded the pair together.

For Rebecca, it was Kevin's random gestures on any given day that showed her she was important to him. For instance, Kevin knew Rebecca's love of the ocean. As a child, she often got to spend time at the ocean when visiting with her grandparents in Florida during the summers. These were some of her best childhood memories. Her grandparents were a constant in providing love and nurturance. The few weeks she would spend with them during the summer were like fuel that powered her through the emotional drain of managing the instability of her normal family life. To Rebecca, her grandparents' unfailing ability to pick up on the little things that were interesting to her made her feel special and seen. One time while at the beach with her grandparents, as Rebecca asked about fish that live in the sea, they explained that starfish had a special ability to repair and regrow missing parts of their extremities when injured. This fascinated Rebecca and only intensified her love for the ocean, its inhabitants, and all the stories behind each as told by her grandparents. One day while they had still been dating, Kevin purchased and surprised Rebecca with a bracelet that had a starfish charm attached. There was no reason, no special occasion, and it was completely unprompted, which made the gift feel even more special. That he remembered her childhood stories of summers with her grandparents made her feel seen and connected. She remembered that feeling. To her, that showed that Kevin was sensitive to her interests, which made her feel loved. For Rebecca, this gift did more in the early years of their relationship than any shortcomings in their relationship. She could always refer back to that moment, memory, and feeling whenever she experienced any disappointments within their relationship. Well, at least she did for a while.

Kevin also had a story of a moment when he had felt his emotional needs had also been met early on in their relationship. Kevin and Rebecca didn't always communicate with one another in their marriage; however, Kevin always admired how well Rebecca seemed to understand him. Many times, he had shared things with her that he had never shared with anyone else. This was really important to Kevin, as he often felt as though he had to shoulder the burden of others when in need. This came from his own childhood. While he had grown up in a two-parent household, Kevin had always seen his father as aloof and uninvolved. He did provide for the family; however, he was never someone Kevin could talk to because of his father's lifelong battle with alcoholism. Instead, Kevin became the proxy man of the house and helped his mother care for the household and his siblings the best way he knew how. He eventually came to understand that his father's addiction and history of childhood trauma had deeply affected his father's parenting. However, he learned early on that the weight of loneliness and disconnection from the strain of this early relationship was too great of a burden to carry himself, so Kevin found himself always searching for a partner with whom he felt he could connect through discussions and dialogue. He loved having the ability to converse with a significant other when in a relationship. He was not interested in superficial dialogue; Kevin always wanted to go deeper. In the deep, Kevin looked for presence. He knew if another individual could meet him here, then he was sure to have a meaningful connection. He knew that with a partner by his side in the deep, he would never be alone again. He had seen that in Rebecca. He told himself that with her, he would finally have someone for him. He knew that if he ever needed someone, she would undoubtedly be by his side.

Near the end of their first session, I was reminded of Rebecca's story about the summers with her grandparents. The idea of regeneration continued to echo in the stories she and Kevin both shared. As they each recounted the issues leading up to the injury in their marriage and now the eventual hope for repair, I thought about how some starfish are able to recover after having experienced trauma and damage to their bodies. The process is not a quick one. In fact, it is believed that sea stars can take up to a year or so to regrow their missing limb. Some are even able to regrow their whole body, as long as a central portion is present. Now Rebecca and Kevin were lying in wait for a similar hope within their marriage as they pursued the process of healing what was central to them both.

As they processed the affair and rehashed their respective emotions attached to the raw wounds, each approached the session with an expressed hope for not only healing but also a new relationship. Rebecca expressed a desire to rebuild trust and strengthen the now much more fragile bond in their marriage. She hoped that her husband would eventually forgive her transgression, as the sinking guilt was almost more than she could bear to stay above as if she was holding just enough air to keep every emotion below her heart. Kevin, on the other hand, not only hoped that he could have trust again in the marriage but also missed having a partner who understood him and yet wondered if he understood or knew Rebecca at all. All that he had known he now questioned. Though he was willing to try and work on the marriage, he secretly wondered if there was anything left to rebuild. If so, it would require a process, one that was steeped in a vision of a healthier marriage and a hope that old things can be made anew, wounds can be healed, and that sometimes broken is just unbroken that is still in development. With time, patience, growth, and appropriate care, what was missing in the marriage, what was taken from the marriage, what was ripped from the marriage, and what may have never been in the marriage, may also possibly be made whole.

Of course, it must be said for this couple that there were and are no guarantees. There are a number of variables that can impact the outcome. Just as the story of sea stars highlights the process of mending, so too will the couple reeling from the effects of an affair on the marriage require a period of intentional time for growth and repair. Again, when the starfish loses a limb, a new one can develop through the process of regeneration. Over time the limb grows to a similar, if not exactly the same size. During the period of growth, the starfish begins to adapt. In time, the process of regeneration completes itself.

We too have restorative capabilities. There exists a process for our deepest emotional traumas, places where trust has been breached and hurt rules. The process of recovery will take some time. The adjustment may be difficult at first. When the mending is complete, however, what remains are the lessons of yesterday and the promise of something completely different, yet new. Some broken promises can be mended.

Your marriage can be healed. However, it will not be an easy process. It will require two people who are dedicated to prioritizing the process of reconnecting the untethered fabric within your relationship.

Imagine the process of shaping and formatting a garment that has been pulled apart. The material may be weathered and thinned, making it more difficult to re-pattern its original format. Perhaps the garment was caught on an object or some other piece of material that caused it to rip and tear. Or maybe the fabric was exposed to a substance that caused a stain that seems irreparable. Similarly, a relationship that has experienced a rip in the fundamental thread of the marriage may often present in a comparative state of disrepair.

The tedious work of attaching and uniting what was once seemingly irrevocably bonded has now also given way to what may at times feel like an overwhelming account of all the damaged and separated parts. In this process, both partners can begin to stitch back the unearthed ruptures in their relationship. They become fine tailors crafting a relationship tapestry made up of different memories, experiences, joys, and challenges. These parts represent a new marriage emerging from the pain of injury.

Respecting the various experiences from the past, this new tapestry encapsulates the journey from past to present and looks toward the future. The process was not simple, but it was not impossible; with the right tools, almost anything can be created in the hands of a skillful holder.

Your relationship will take daily work. Think back to our analogy of the employee earlier in this chapter. If you recall, we discussed how work in the marriage can be seen as analogous to work on the job. The only difference here is that you are employed by the marriage. Daily you will want to arrive with the disposition of having prepared for the skill-demanding tasks and duties that you accepted in this role of your relationship. Your position will require expertise and continual training in order to remain competent and stay current with the growth trends in your marriage. There will be specific goals, and they will need to be evaluated in order to track the state of your relationship. You may even consider hiring an outside source to provide counsel and consultation on this specific project you and your spouse are working on: your affair recovery. This work is not for the faint of heart. You may want to quit your job—the marriage—at times.

Like Rebecca and Kevin, you will wonder if there is anything left for you in your role within the marriage. You may have moments of deep despair, shame, and loneliness as well as high moments of hope and excitement. This roller coaster of emotions can cause you to constantly question your ability to do the work as you endeavor within the marriage.

Like your job, when the performance goals and strategies for your role have not benefited the project or organization, you find yourself wondering if you have what it takes to fulfill the requirements. Conversely, when the feedback and proof of implementation in your daily tasks begin to yield the desired outcome to the project or work in the organization, you find yourself feeling more securely positioned for the tasks ahead.

This approach to your marriage will also allow you to confidently establish a course for recovery and healing in your marriage. Understanding the rigorous nature of relationship reconciliation and affair recovery is key to approaching the journey with all the necessary tools to successfully meet the demands of your marriage goals.

The work will be daily. It will require consistency. It will require education and periodic evaluation. It will feel repetitive and monotonous at times. Yet there will be unexpected moments as well. In all of this, it will require patience and dedication in order to pursue all of the other tenets necessary to repairing the relationship.

By now you may be wondering whether the work required to restore the relationship to health and connectedness is even worth it. Maybe the question being asked is much more personal. Perhaps you wonder whether or not you still have desire for your partner and if your partner still has desire for you. This is a fundamental question that every spouse must answer. Only you will know the answer. You may even need to take time to process your own personal individual goals and reflect on them in light of the broader life plan you currently have in place for yourself. This is no different than any other role we accept in life—we frequently find ourselves making selections in life from a fundamental core belief. What are yours? Where do they fit in this space of reflection within your marriage?

Once you center on the answers and you know the orientation from which every direction follows with assurance, then you can embark upon the journey to reconcile your relationship bond. It is this assurance that provides the wellspring of sheer hope steadily moving you and your partner toward the vision and goal of a healthy and healed marriage.

CHAPTER 2

NAVIGATING PANIC AND FEAR

When a partner has been unfaithful, it can oftentimes feel like an unexpected disaster. It's as if one minute you're sleeping and the next you wake up with the house on fire. This sudden activation of your internal alert system, which one moment before was at rest, can be startling and confusing, leaving you panic-stricken. Managing the sudden onslaught of ranging emotions can be traumatic.

In fact, for many the experience of navigating the response to perceived emotional danger is frequently described as trauma. This may come as a surprise to some. Finding out your partner has had an affair and the way in which the mind processes this information can be very traumatizing. Of course, discovering that someone you trust had betrayed your confidence would be painful for anyone.

The difference in using the word *trauma* here is the degree of effect on the emotional and physiological system. Merriam-Webster's Dictionary defines *trauma* as: "1) a disordered psychic or behavioral state resulting from severe mental or emotional stress or physical injury, or 2) an emotional upset."[2] Trauma can be any emotionally upsetting event, especially one that has caused one's physiological, emotional, and physical response system to react in unhealthy, irregular ways.

In other words, when a person has experienced an emotionally and/or physically upsetting event, it can be destabilizing to their overall approach in managing moments of distress and conflict. The way that thoughts and feelings are experienced can be thrown into an emotional blender of sorts, like a frenzied stirring of emotions as you begin your attempts to make sense of the events that have occurred in your marriage. It is this intrapsychic experience of disorderly and dysregulated chaos that causes panic and increased fear where once abided safety, security, regularity, and normality. Not having this sense of normality and sameness can be very disconcerting.

Normality is not viewed here as a social construct but instead as an internal entity of the inner and personal world that lives in and around you. It is the proverbial lens through which you filter information and develop boundaries, rules, and expectations. Normal is relative; what may be standard for one person may not be for another. However, these individualized intrapsychic patterns and expectations often provide a sense of emotional safety. Again, what internalized reality may look like for one may look different for another, but our minds naturally seek out emotional and physical spaces that cultivate a sense of safety and security.[3] Normality provides that for us.

Normality helps us to understand our world and make sense of new material.[4] In fact, your brain is wired to take data and integrate it into existing knowledge. This is a necessary function, as we would be overwhelmed with the amount of information we consistently encounter without having a quasi-receivable sorting and storage mechanism in our brain. However, when there are disruptions in the long-established processes within our minds, they may cause structural changes in the system that can subsequently create interruptions in the entire system.

Within your mind, there exists a process for knowledge integration within yourself, your relationships, and the broader world around you. When that process experiences a disruption, the impact can be seen in other components of the system. When what was normal, sure, consistent, regulated, and orderly becomes unsure, disordered, dysregulated, inconsistent, and abnormal In our lives, it would make sense that there would be resulting stress to our internal psychological systems. The longer the interruptions exist, the more it stands to reason how profoundly significant the consequences to one's established internal model would be.

Understanding this helps us to see how disruptions in the relationship system for connection, bonding, and trust have the capability to reverberate in pervasive ways. It is these reverberations in the relationship system that echo the groundswells of anxiety, fear, confusion, and sadness all at once. The cascading emotions build with varying degrees of momentum while collecting particle thoughts and reminders along the way until the wave of panic washes over. The waves wash over sometimes unexpectedly and sometimes you can see them far off.

Perhaps it is knowing the submersion is approaching that makes it much more difficult. Or perhaps it is the unexpected increase in the size of the panic wave. Wherever you fall on the spectrum, understanding the mind and body's system response to experiencing what is perceived as a threatening or stressful event will be key to your eventual emotional recovery.

Anatomy of Fear in Marriage

Let's discuss the mind and body's process for processing a threatening event. This is our physiological and psychological response to stressors that we perceive pose a threat to our physical or emotional environment. This response is a well-coordinated series of physiological activations initiated to alert us to danger and the need for a protective act. These key processes are necessary to our survival as a species and are evolutionary in nature.[5] This means that these processes are intrinsic for all of us and serve a functional purpose to mankind specifically in that the internal mechanisms are there to assist us with surviving perceived life-threatening and dangerous situations. The processes set off an organized physiological sequence of biologically wired steps to assist us with surviving threats or dangerous events. This biologically wired sequence is often described as the fight-or-flight response, where when faced with danger, terror, and threat, we are subsequently able to fight off or flee danger.[6] The brain is essentially alerted to prepare biological systems for protection to threats of safety and security. What happens within the body and mind to prepare for this sequence of events is a combination of responses beginning with sensory input. When this information is received, it then is sent "to the amygdala, an area of the brain that contributes to emotional processing. The amygdala interprets images and sounds. When it perceives danger, it instantly sends a distress signal to the hypothalamus."[7] This area of the brain functions like a command center, communicating with the rest of the body through the nervous system so that the person has the energy to fight or flee."[8]

After the alert has been activated, the nervous system subsequently triggers a concert of physical and chemical reactions. These reactions work alongside other bodily systems to help secure access to internal resources which ensure safety and protection against threat and injury. The musculoskeletal, respiratory, cardiovascular, endocrine, and gastrointestinal systems then begin to leverage their synergy to assist the individual in escaping a dangerous scenario.

Let's take a closer look at the internal systems within the body. In the musculoskeletal system, the muscles may tense up with stress, often an immediate reaction. The respiratory system provides oxygen to various parts of the body along with removing toxic carbon dioxide. This process also provides needed oxygen to blood cells that aid in circulation. This may manifest as rapid breathing while your body prepares for its next coordinated response in the chain of protection and defense. Additionally, your cardiovascular system is increasing blood flow and may express itself as an increased heart rate. The hormone-producing endocrine system is made up of glands that house and produce the required hormones to initiate the alert response. Within the endocrine system lies the hypothalamus. "The hypothalamus, a collection of nuclei that connects the brain and the endocrine system, signals the pituitary gland to produce a hormone, which in turn signals the adrenal glands, located above the kidneys, to increase the production of cortisol."[9] The hormone cortisol then provides fuel for the activation of needed energy throughout the body. Next, digestion begins to slow in order to consolidate energy, which will be used for the broader response to looming danger.

These systemic responses make up the fight-or-flight response, one regulated by the overall nervous system, which includes the autonomic and somatic nervous systems. Within the autonomic nervous system, you find comprised within vital networks that engage the sympathetic nervous system (SNS) and the parasympathetic nervous system (PNS). It is this circuitry between both systems which works to prepare and return the individual to a corresponding level of threat responses based on perceived data. Let's take a closer look at this process.

"The SNS signals the adrenal glands to release hormones called adrenaline (epinephrine) and cortisol. These hormones, together with direct actions of autonomic nerves, cause the heart to beat faster, respiration rate to increase, blood vessels in the arms and legs to dilate, digestive process to change and glucose levels (sugar energy) in the bloodstream t to increase to respond to the emergency. The SNS response needs to be fairly sudden to prepare the body to respond to an emergency situation or acute stress—short-term stressors. Once the crisis is over, the body usually returns to the pre-emergency, unstressed state. This recovery is facilitated by the PNS, which generally has opposing effects to the SNS."[10]

It is the facilitation of the PNS that allows us to recover from the instinctive nervous system threat response to danger. Once the incoming data received is no longer interpreted as dangerous, the PNS then allows the other internal systems to return to homeostasis, where emotional, chemical and bodily functions engage the environment with "rest and digest" responses.[11]

Now that your body and mind are no longer confronting threats to safety and security, you are able to access incoming information in ways that facilitate healthy emotional and behavioral reactions. No longer fearing the inevitable, your body and mind have responsive flexibility. The environment seems much calmer, and because of this, the ways in which you will respond are much clearer. Instead of solely relying on instinctive primal and emotional parts of the mind, the rational parts of the mind can work in concert as well. This choreography of function allows the individual to detect nuance, context, needs, and desires, and to pursue them in ways that eventually lead to a healthy resolution of distress. In other words, knowing when you are actively engaged in a fight-or-flight response to what may otherwise be common stressors within any relationship can help you address and resolve moments of relational distress while minimizing the risk of profound injury to one another in your attempt to escape the perceived crisis of emotional danger. Knowing when your nervous system response is activated—in what I reference sometimes as "The Bear"—and when instead you can see that you are simply face-to-face with your partner will create a hierarchy of moving through conflict. The Bear must be faced or evaded before you and your partner are able to engage one another during conflict where each of you can do so in ways where you still feel connected and attached.

The following section takes you on an imaginary journey through a fear activation and the body's possible response. The text is written as a tool for guided imagery as well, which we discuss later in the book. In this scenario, we use this narrative as an invitation to imagine physiological responses that may occur if we were truly in this fictitious story.

For some of you, simply reading this will trigger a protective response and heightened arousal depending on your personal trauma history. As with anything, proceed with caution and certainly feel free to skip to the next section.

This portion of the text is meant to illustrate an example of how one might move through perceived impending danger in order to key in individual responses that may also show up in moments of perceived emotional threat within your marriage.

Let's take a tour by way of imagery to better understand this detail of distress and our physiological response to it.

Guided through Fear: A Visualization

Imagine you are on a pasture of green land for as far as the eye can see. The sun is shining brightly. It is early summer and the temperature is still cool, but there is an emerging pinch of heat on the skin where the sun directs its rays. It doesn't hurt but rather wakes you up to the moment—the more pinching, the more waking. You see everything around you. You feel the wind as it caresses your face. It is subtle so you miss it at first. Then a moment later you pick up the sweet notes of summer's garden whirling all around you. You are walking. You hear the birds' vocals, and without words every so often you discern their chatter. It's quiet outside, but if you listen hard enough, you realize just how loud everything you sense outside really is. It's loud, but it's rhythmic, organized—every sound has a purpose, every smell comes from a place, everything seen has its own unique prescribed position, and everything felt comes as no surprise.

Until there is a disturbance. Something in the rhythm seems out of tune. There is a sound that seems a little off. It's not loud enough yet to warrant any massive response but still different enough that you notice. You are walking, but instead of looking trustingly and assuredly straight ahead, your senses become more heightened, almost as if there were a volume function for each perceptive organ. You start listening sensitively, sensing more keenly. Lacking additional feedback, you continue on while attempting to rationalize the brief interruption. In your inner world, you find yourself relaxing back into the comfort of knowing and the ways in which you know.

Suddenly again there is something different. This time it is an unfamiliar noise behind you. Not rhythmic—this sound is unfamiliar and incoherent. Although not loud enough that anyone else around would necessarily hear, it is loud enough to register. While perceptions remain heightened, the proverbial volume function is up, yet you see nothing. What's more, the sound has now retreated. There is no loud disruption, there is nothing to see. Everything seems normal, yet nothing feels normal. Inside yourself, there is a sinking feeling in your gut as if it is tied to a rope. Your heart begins to flutter and the speed is not quite rapid, but you feel it has increased. It's harder to see the things around you because everything in front of you seems clouded. You try to make sense of this unknown noise that seemingly stalks you yet is nowhere to be found.

You try to investigate with your thoughts, thinking of what it is and what you should do. The answers arise like a magic ball, where asking seems just as futile as receiving the direct answer in the way that they both fade in and out. This is because your mind feels clouded too. Still, nothing is there to warrant any change from which you are protecting yourself. You feel anxious, confused, and afraid. You want to protect yourself, but still you are unsure of the threat. So you keep walking.

This time the evidence begins to mount. There is certainly something there. The sounds come in more clearly. There is a new rhythm. In fact, what was once unrecognizable starts to organize into an undeniable picture. More than wind, you notice there is a galloping happening behind you. The wind is flowing differently around you, and the inhabitants of the earth are suddenly communicating something different. This time you tell yourself that when you turn around, you will undoubtedly discover the reality of what you had perceived. There was a threat on the horizon.

Now the threat is upon you. You are terrified and excited at the same time. The excitement is not of happiness but one of preparedness. You ready yourself for what is now certainly behind you. For some, a growing urge to run away may be your initial instinctive response. The fear is insurmountable, and all you can think to do is escape the fear of what is to come. Due to the excitement, you perhaps may instead instinctively prepare to fight. Your body becomes warm, and your extremities activate with energy. You can feel your heart pumping the blood flow with speed to all the important appendages.

They will help you handle the attack while protecting yourself. Or finally, you may want to do both: fight and flee. Filled with a burst of excitement, fear, and anxiety, you find yourself torn between both responses. It is not quite that you find yourself evaluating the efficacy of either approaches, to run or to fight. Rather, it is your automatic nervous system's trigger to an overwhelming threat that sets off a simultaneous response to both aforementioned positions. In other words, you find yourself wanting to both fight and flee.

This leads to a paralysis of motion where technically you are moving but parts of you are moving in opposing directions. This opposing tension forces you to remain right where you are. Now with a burgeoning primal desire to protect yourself from the onslaught of impending danger, you turn around. In the field, you discover that behind you is your worst fear come true.

It is *The Bear*.

The Bear may take on many different meanings. In marriage, The Bear may be divorce or abandonment. For others, it may mean not being seen as worthy or accepted or more. The key is in knowing what The Bear, or rather your worst fears come true, looks like to you.

Now, standing face-to-face with your opponent, you find yourself doing before thinking and feeling before fully knowing. How would you respond? Would you fight, flee, or freeze?

Now imagine what it would be like to process, articulate, and express your thoughts with another during this heightened moment of distress. In other words, imagine having to conduct a conversation with your spouse about relational distress all the while responding to and managing the physiological threat alert your body has now engaged. You can see your partner. You may even be able to decipher sounds, but your attention is most certainly focused on the ominous threat that surrounds you.

This, of course, is just an analogy to describe and better understand ourselves when responding to marital distress during communication and when perceiving the moment as dangerous, threatening, and/or emotionally unsafe. Yet this scenario is an all-too-familiar pattern in many marriages. We often find ourselves attempting to engage with our partners, whom we love and cherish, the most during moments of physiological terror. You think you are only having a conversation with your partner, when in reality your body is also simultaneously fighting The Bear.

Talking To Your Loving Partner while Fighting The Bear

What is it like speaking with your partner when your nervous system is in battle mode? Think back to the last argument you had with your partner. What was the issue? Think back to what you were feeling when you sensed the argument brewing. Were you anxious? Did you feel returning exhaustion, as if immediately you had run a marathon and were now out of breath? Were you angry? Did you feel afraid? Remember the moments when you were experiencing the emotions and how these feelings were punctuated during certain parts of the argument. For instance, what happened to you when your partner raised their voice? What emotions did you feel? How about when they seemed to emotionally shut down, or perhaps when they left the room of the argument; what did you feel then? Maybe it was certain words that were said or facial expressions that caused the feeling of fear to grip your body.

Now take a moment and think of the thoughts that were racing through your mind at that moment. What did you tell yourself? How did you respond to the thoughts? What did you feel in response to the thoughts? Consider all the thoughts, feelings, and behaviors that occurred during the argument.

Sometimes another way to view these moments is to imagine yourself as an outside observer looking in at the moment of conflict. Can you see yourself now? If so, consider how your response may have been affected by the near certain emotional distress you were experiencing during the conflict. Perhaps as the noise level increased, your tone did as well. The way your partner approached you may have been followed by your response in leaving the room. Did they follow? If so, you might have stayed to argue your case or perhaps ceased all eye contact and communication.

The more you observe now, the more you begin to see how intertwined your emotional and cognitive responses are with that of your physiology when activated during perceived threats. These excitatory responses are a glimpse into what happens when you are fighting The Bear while attempting to have very nuanced conversations with your loving partner, complete with heightened attention to behaviors, verbal, and nonverbal cues. Much of your blood flow is moving to preparing systems of your body to respond to danger, terror, The Bear, and your spouse. Remember that physiologically, your body's nervous system is wired for this defensive and protective mechanism. The more astute you are in acknowledging this symbiotic dynamic, the better able you are to decipher temporary stressors in your marriage from real moments of danger.

Rebecca and Kevin learned this the hard way. Kevin began to share during sessions that he would often find himself shutting down or, as he described, turning off. He described how during conflict or how sometimes at the hint of conflict, he would begin to feel frustration, annoyance, and irritation. Eventually, he later would find that underneath the frustration was sadness that would ultimately revisit after many arguments as he wished that his partner would understand him and his needs. Additionally, Kevin learned that his physiology during relational distress told a story as well. He began to understand how his body responded to stress and the emotional threat during the argument. For instance, he stated that his heart would race so fast that it would cause his glands to excrete more sweat. He also explained that while on the outside he may seem cool and collected, inside there was a building churn in the pit of his stomach. Kevin shared that when Rebecca started to sum up his thoughts and statements, it was a sign that Rebecca was ready to move on from the conversation. More than moving on, Kevin believed Rebecca would rather have not been bothered with his needs at all. Though Rebecca never directly said this, Kevin believed it. It was this belief that would dominate his mind during arguments with her. Like an old friend who visits frequently, comfortably, and maybe without notice, these thoughts would return each time an argument began to ensue. Like clockwork, physiological activation, the thoughts, the feelings, and then the behavioral response would arrive at its usual time. In this case, the eventual shutting down and turning off for Kevin would occur whenever he felt the overwhelming sensation of not being heard and the hopelessness in not having his needs met within the marriage.

Rebecca was partly the same but a little different. Rebecca would immediately begin to feel anxious and sad at the onset of an argument. Rebecca admitted that while she might be smiling on the outside, on the inside she was anything but. She would explain that she feared arguments could escalate and lead to bigger issues in the relationship. They could lead to the kind of issues in relationships she had witnessed growing up, ones where partners are interchangeable and relationships are never permanent. She feared that they were always one big argument from calling it quits. Rebecca didn't always say that during arguments, but it was always in the back of her mind. That thought would come with strong feelings during conflict. She would often feel tremendous anxiety, fear, and sadness. She saw herself as the one burdened with saving the relationship and always fixing things when there was something wrong. It wasn't that Kevin ever directly told her that it was her responsibility, but it seemed to her that that responsibility was a given for her. So she accepted it, because if not her, then who? No one. At least that is what she told herself. Without her, the marriage could easily devolve to separation and ultimately divorce. This was the last thing Rebecca wanted, and it was her greatest fear during each and every big argument.

Once Rebecca and Kevin were able to begin the work of separating their moments of panic and fear from their wants and needs during relationship distress and conflict, they were better able to minimize and resolve their momentary physiological responses. This proved to be invaluable to the couple as they attempted to communicate through distressing moments. Understanding how their body's responses to stress and fear aided their ability to calm intensely felt emotions, ones which before had often been experienced negatively. Their fear, anxiety, and sadness were no longer the predominant emotions leading the default array of responses when facing perceived emotional terror and threat.

Armed with the knowledge of how their threat responses impacted their protective response, they were now able to ask for what they needed. Interestingly enough, that new ability actually helped them to get their needs met. When they no longer had to focus on psychological protections, this freed them to focus on unmet needs and better ways to pursue their likelihood of being met. They learned to differentiate relational distress and perceived attacks from emotional fears and longings for one another. Their partner had in essence become the figurehead or symbolic threat to emotional safety and security. Now they could separate their loving partner from The Bear, which represented emotional threat during challenges to the relationships. This made triggering moments less emotionally reactive for the individual partners and within the broader dynamic in the relationship. Instead of attacking one another, they could face their fears together. There would be no running away now. There would also be no charging toward what might look like the last great battle. There would be no immobility because the direction for defeat was now known. Instead, they would remain calm and try not to panic, speak softly to one another but stand their ground. They recognized that their true opponent was the unhealthy response to a genuine need and not their loving partner. They could minimize the danger of The Bear's presence without fearing the risk of emotional attack from each other. It would require knowing their triggers for perceived threats, managing their physiological and emotional responses, and understanding the underlying psychological activation and drive. It would be like knowing when you and your spouse are in bear country and are prepared and aware enough to tread skillfully, slowly, and safely with one another.

Writing Prompt

Take a moment to determine and jot down what your responses are when you perceive an argument stirring with your partner. Perhaps you will find that the arguments are more of a peak emotional experience because you find yourself regularly activated in the valley of emotional triggers. Either way, it will be important to know and map what your emotions, behaviors, and physiology look like when facing and responding to negative moments within the marriage.

CHAPTER 3

"IS THIS NORMAL?"

During a session, Kevin reported seeing himself as different after discovering the affair in his marriage. He shared that while he knew that he and his wife had communication challenges within the marriage and other occasional issues had arisen from time to time, his marriage was like many typical marriages. He knew it wasn't perfect and that it was unrealistic to assume perfection from one another. In fact, he often reported that he would just let conflicts in the marriage go without mention. He did this knowing that, in spite of what he called "hiccups of relationships," they were committed to one another. He never questioned their commitment to one another. Sure, he felt misunderstood, unheard, and lonely at times when issues would develop in the marriage, but even with these issues he shared in the session, he never believed infidelity would ever be one of them. In fact, he said it was the one thing he knew for sure would never happen in his marriage.

This is what made the shock of learning about the affair a profound event—a seismic internal shift that reverberated to the core of who he was and everything that he thought he knew. The aftershocks would seem chaotic to Kevin. There were times when he could expect them and times when they were sudden. Something in the environment would remind him of some part of the pain that he carried. They would come in the form of questions, emotions, behaviors, and thoughts. They would pertain to the affair specifically and sometimes seem unrelated, but with deeper investigation, there would most certainly be a connection. This was one of the most frustrating parts of the affair recovery for Kevin. He had already decided to forgive his partner and move forward, yet he would find the after-effects of the affair permeating many facets of his life. The questions, feelings, and behaviors had him frequently asking "Is it normal?" as a result of the ways he responded to the trauma of having discovered a fracture in his internal schema of life and love.

I explained to Kevin that it was important to differentiate between the concept of normal and abnormal and introduced the notion of what can be common in response to the disruption of normal.

For instance, Kevin shared that he often wondered whether it was normal to find himself periodically questioning details pertaining to his wife's sexual experience with her affair partner. He stated that it was not that he truly wanted to know the details; it was that he wanted to know how he could have missed not knowing. How he did not notice when his partner was gone for long hours at work in order to complete projects? He has thought since then that those were the moments she was with the affair partner: the times she would pick up the phone and leave the room, only to return with an announcement she had errands to run at the grocery store, the gym, or some other urgent last-minute task. He now knew those were times she was with him. How could he have been so sure that there was nothing amiss, he wondered to himself and now aloud in session? He asked himself time and time again: how could he have not known until he knew?

Once he knew, he had to know everything. Kevin often processed in session his sometimes-fervent focus on understanding every piece of information in his mind as it related to the affair. He often described the knowledge he possessed about infidelity as a disorganized puzzle of one million pieces. From far away, he felt the task seemed immensely overwhelming, but each connected piece fueled his hunger to make sense of the picture. Kevin said he "had to know" the details in order to make sense of the past and eventually trust this new reality of rebuilding in the marriage by seeing things as they truly were.

This required deep intrapsychic work on the part of both Kevin and his partner to learn and communicate what their deep attachment triggers and needs were, as we will discuss in Chapter 4, when we discuss attachment and bonding (as coined by well-known psychiatrist and researcher John Bowlby). Doing so helped them both to communicate their truest desires with one another in their quest for obtaining love and belonging, but incidentally also aided in their ability to reorganize negative stories they had come to believe about their partnership. They learned that it was not that their partner was intentionally withholding these longings, but that oftentimes there was a series of factors that impeded their ability to truly know and meet each other's needs.

Understanding the Injured and the Injurer

For purposes of clarity, we will refer to the person who had been cheated on as the injured and the person who cheated as the injurer. Please do not delve too deeply into the assigned labels. They are only labels and they are meant to decipher the varying degrees of response each partner may have after the discovery of the affair. These labels are not to assume that there has not been an occurrence of injury on both sides. I highlight the differences simply to explain commonalities that may occur when one has been cheated on and the other has done the cheating. This is not a definitive description. However, looking at common responses may help answer what may sometimes feel like unique reactions, which are many times experienced in isolation. When this happens, you may find yourself frequently asking, "Is this normal?" Now, let's first take a look at the injured.

The Injured

When the injured affair partner has discovered that their spouse has cheated, the flood of emotions that begin to arise can feel overwhelming and breathtaking. This moment can sometimes feel debilitating in the immediate aftermath of discovering the affair. Though initially dubbed the moment you found out about the affair, it can quickly become what seems like an entire life lived in that space of time. You will never forget that moment of confluence when research, questions, emotion, thought, and your corresponding action merged and became what is now the moment of discovery.

Like a compass navigating you through the storm waters, so will this moment be a reference point you will frequently refer to in moments of relational distress. Unlike a compass, when you discover the affair, the moment will not be a guide for you to help determine your next steps; rather it will compel you toward acts of self-preservation when triggers are activated and panic has set in. While we are not speaking specifically about clinical panic and anxiety disorders—which may sometimes occur during an overall clinical approach to treating the trauma and aftermath of affair recovery—the general focus here is on the individual who has just discovered the affair and the ensuing questions and actions that may occur after learning of such.

Let's take a look at common questions you may ask yourself after the affair:

1. Will I ever be able to trust my partner?
2. Can I ever trust anyone?
3. Who else knew?
4. How could I not know?
5. Does and did my spouse ever love me?
6. Can I trust myself?
7. Does anyone understand what I am experiencing?
8. Will I have to pretend for family and/or friends?
9. Will life ever be the same?
10. Does my spouse find me attractive?
11. How can I still love someone who has betrayed me?
12. How can there be any intimacy?
13. How can in one moment I love my spouse and in the next feel nothing?
14. Does my spouse still think about the affair partner?
15. Does my spouse love the affair partner?
16. Does my spouse still want to be married?
17. Am I stupid for even considering working on your marriage?
18. Am I letting someone take advantage of my love?
19. Is my spouse still communicating with the affair partner?
20. What was intimacy like between the affair partner and my spouse?
21. Am I to blame? Is something wrong with me?
22. Is my spouse not who I thought they were?

23. Should I keep the affair secret?

24. What are the dates pertaining to the affair (i.e., time it started, ended, trips, etc.)?

25. Will my spouse eventually leave even though they're staying right now?

Cycling through the thoughts and emotions, you may feel as though you are in a never-ending spinning wheel. Though exhausted by questions, you may also find yourself energized in pursuit of finding the right answer. Not any answer will do. You will be looking for the right answer, not knowing what that answer you earnestly seek will truly be, at least initially. The answers will be satisfying once the questions become much clearer and succinct. Instead of focusing on the periphery of your marriage's journey to betrayal, you will see that the questions were essentially clues from your heart destined toward the space required for relational healing and repair. It is here that both the question and the desired answer originate. It will take time and intentional inner work to be able to locate this space.

Though this phase may feel confusing, disorienting, and disorganized, know that these questions, emotions, and genuine responses lead you to the eventual reorientation, emotional reorganization, and cognitive restructuring necessary for mending and integrating the wounds of your past.

The Injurer

Rebecca had a different response to the affair injury within the relationship. Instead of the constant questioning of whether or not a responsive behavior, thought, or emotion was to be expected after the affair, Rebecca only expressed a few questions. In fact, Rebecca carried what seemed to be a resolute acceptance of her position. Essentially, she believed that the current distress in the marriage all boiled down to one truth: it was all her fault.

This sense that the current problems of the marriage were a direct result of her infidelity led Rebecca to often carry tremendous feelings of guilt, shame, embarrassment, and sadness. Even saying the words *infidelity*, *affair*, and *cheating* aloud was hard. Rebecca would rather have said any other word than the exact thing she knew it to be. Hearing those words aloud brought Rebecca back to the guilt, shame, embarrassment, and sadness. It is not as if she had never experienced these feelings, albeit in another context and with other people throughout her lifetime; it was that these feelings echoed deep throughout the corridors of her heart.

These subsequent emotions from the affair carried a weight that seemed to create a drag on any forward movement. The weight was like chains sometimes, constraining Rebecca to a potential lifetime of confinement—a life in which she would always be seen as the guilty perpetrator who had committed terrible crimes against the marriage and her partner. However, Rebecca would often describe the weight as too much to bear. Indeed, these emotions were all-consuming, and yet to the external observer it would seem as though everything was fine. Rebecca shared how she would often push the weight down so deep that what remained was a hollow hole within. She said she needed to do this in order to not succumb to the disappointment and self-loathing she sometimes struggled with. She was determined not to fully feel these emotions because she felt if she did, all that was good within her might not make it back.

Even more prominent than the guilt, shame, embarrassment, and sadness was the fear. Rebecca feared that if she believed everything she told herself, the negative thoughts would consume the remaining good she possessed. She had to believe she was good and that she was worthy. These were thoughts she had fought since watching her parents' revolving door of relationships, sometimes wondering if she had been at fault. If she had been a better stepdaughter, less needy, more responsible, less emotional, maybe things in her life would have been different. Fearing this question again, now as she stood on one side of the marriage chasm, stretching as far as the eye can perceive, she wondered the same thing again. She wondered now—if only she had not been needy, emotional, if she had been more independent, would her marriage now be on the brink of collapse?

Instead of pondering the answer and instead of nearing collapse, she told herself she would hold up the weight by being strong, stoic even. She would take whatever her partner had to throw at her. She would not share her emotions because she would instead be there to accept all of Kevin's. Instead of expressing her needs, she would push them down because his needs would be more important. When she would feel her emotions and needs arise, she would ignore them, because what was most important for her was maintaining what was already a fragile and thinly layered bond.

In order to avert this possibility, she would find herself instead:

1. Shielding negative emotions in order to avoid additional negative repercussions.

2. Avoiding conversations about the affair.

3. Distracting Kevin from affair-related conversations in order to quell possible partner triggers that might remind him of the affair.

4. Being abundantly transparent to thwart possible interrogating questions pertaining to the affair.

5. Being easily defensive because of the enormous emotional weight of having caused her partner pain.

6. Being easily angered during discussions of the affair when the efforts of fixing the relationship seemed momentarily dashed by the renewed realization of her partner's deep emotional wounds.

7. Planning recreational activities to find ways to fix problems of the relationship connection within the marriage.

8. Working more than normal as a result of wanting to avoid the negative emotions.

9. Spending more time with friends in order to balance the negative affections of her marriage with more positive ones in other friendships.

10. Omitting words in conversations related to the affair because of the disappointment and other negative reminders relating to her personhood.

What Rebecca later realized in sessions with her partner was that each time she pushed her emotions down, she would push her partner away. To Kevin, it seemed as though she did not care. Sure, there would be moments when she would discuss her thoughts about what became known as "the incident," but she would rarely share her deep inner feelings about the affair. It wasn't that she never thought about it. It was exactly the opposite: she thought about it all the time. On the inside, she was managing the pressure of exposing her emotions. She was constantly trying to not yield to the overflowing feeling of sadness and self-disappointment. If she did, the wreckage could be great. She could trigger an avalanche of negative emotions from her partner, which could lead to damage beyond repair—or so she feared.

While these were common questions and behaviors for our example couple, it is important to note that every couple is different. That is because every individual is different. We each bring our own unique perspective, background, and experiences to every relationship. This in turn causes responses to discovering and beginning the process of healing from marital infidelity to vary.

It is helpful to have as a backdrop the more common responses from others who have also gone before you in this journey. It will be equally important to recall that your marital journey toward healing will be unique to you. Understanding this will help you find comfort in knowing that you are not alone. At the same time, knowing that your journey belongs to you and your partner will hopefully help you find acceptance for the directions in which this process will take you both.

Writing Prompt

Take a moment to determine and jot down what pattern of behaviors you have observed in response to the affair. What questions do you find yourself frequently asking? Perhaps you know that you are grappling with specific negative beliefs pertaining to the affair and are unsure what they are. Take some time to reflect without personal judgement as a way to better understand what your adaptive responses have been to the marital affair.

CHAPTER 4

MARRIAGE BONDING

Early on during the intake process for both Kevin and Rebecca, they had provided information about the number of children they both shared. Rebecca noted that when she had had her first child, there had been some initial complications during the delivery. Everything eventually worked out, and her child was healthy and is thriving today. However, the transition from delivery to birth was a difficult process and one she shared that she would never forget.

During the final stage of delivery, Rebecca's daughter's heartbeat began to drop with each contraction. Initially, the doctors believed it was normal and to be expected, as this can sometimes happen during contractions. They assured her that as long as the heart rate returned to normal in between the intervals, there was no reason to be concerned. However, as any expectant mother would, Rebecca paid close attention to the heart rate each time she contracted and pushed. Progressively, the baby's heart rate became more irregular and eventually the doctors confirmed her suspicion that her baby may be in distress. With the help of quick medical intervention, she soon thereafter delivered a healthy baby girl. The medical team discovered that her baby had a mild umbilical cord compression that had begun to constrain the baby's access to oxygen during labor and delivery. Those few moments after her birth were the longest moments of Rebecca's life, wondering if there was anything wrong with her baby—or worse, would she survive? It was an unimaginable fear. When her daughter finally began to breathe, deep relief rushed through Rebecca, like having sipped from a bottle filled with an elixir, wiping all negative emotion and memory away. Rebecca's baby had been placed on her chest, and that was all she had known in the moment. When the doctors laid the baby on her bosom, she had immediately locked eyes with her daughter. They had gazed at one another, and she had known instantly that they belonged to one another. She had felt her daughter lay across her skin and absorbed her warmth and in exchange, Rebecca had found rest and peace in now knowing that everything was going to be okay. This was an instant connection. This was bonding.

John Bowlby was a well-known researcher and psychoanalyst who created the work of *attachment theory* shortly after graduating from Cambridge University. The primary underpinning of attachment theory is its "focus on the biological bases of attachment behavior."[12] As *The Handbook of Attachment* explains, "Attachment behavior has the predictable outcome of increasing proximity of the child to the attachment figures."[13] This constant assessment in determining proximity and closeness to a primary attachment figure, which is most notably documented between a mother and child, is an innate mechanism for organizing attachment within cognitive, behavioral, social, and evolutionary survivalist constructs.

Developmental psychologist, colleague, and researcher Mary Salter Ainsworth contributed to this theory by observing differences in affectional bonds through naturalistic observation studies in both Uganda in the 1950s and Baltimore, Maryland in the 1960s. Ainsworth later created an assessment tool called the "Strange Situation." That triggered the productive flowering of the foundational study of individual differences of attachment quality. Ainsworth also further developed the idea of affectional bonds that reflect "the attraction that one individual has for another individual."[14] When this individual is experiencing distress, they also pursue and possess the ability to seek and obtain a sense of security within a relationship they perceive as secure. The behaviors that serve as the varying behavioral systems for attachment are referred to as *attachment behaviors*. Ainsworth noted that there were "individual differences in attachment qualities," which involve "proximity maintenance and separation protest" toward the establishment of a secure base from which the world is explored and where one can obtain comfort in times of threat.[15] These attachment qualities can be described as secure (as described earlier in our text) or insecure, the latter of which denotes fear and uncertainty about being able to pursue and obtain proximity to the attachment figure upon experienced and perceived threats to security.

There are several types of attachment engagements. However, for our purposes we will focus primarily on the attempts an individual makes, or rather the attachment behaviors one displays, in order to obtain proximity or protest separation. *The Handbook of Attachment* explains these behaviors in the following way:

> Attachment Theory also suggests a link between the quality of infant attachment relationships and subsequent adult attachment relationships. Bowlby proposed that during the years of "immaturity" (infancy to adolescence), individuals gradually develop expectations of attachment figures, based on experiences with these individuals. Expectations about the availability and responsiveness of attachment figures are incorporated into "working models" which guide perceptions and behavior in later relationships.[16]

This is important, as it seems that our early working models of attachment in relationship to our initial primary caregiver can shed light on the ways in which we engage in primary attachments in adult relationships, including our romantic relationships. Cindy Hazan and Phillip Shaver, authors of "Romantic Love Conceptualized as an Attachment Process," noted this in their research, where they proposed that "romantic love could be conceptualized as an attachment process," where three styles of attachment patterning emerge similarly to attachment in infancy.[17] These attachment patterns are secure, anxious-ambivalent, and avoidant. The latter two patterns would be characterized as an insecure attachment engagement, as we discussed earlier in the chapter. Additional researchers by the names of K. Bartholomew and L.M. Horowitz "subsequently proposed a four-group model of adult attachment based on Bowlby's claim that attachment patterns reflect working models of self and others."[18] These four categories are secure, anxious-preoccupied, dismissive-avoidant, and fearful-avoidant. Bartholomew and Horowitz asserted that models of self can be dichotomized as positive or negative (the self is seen as either worthy of love and attention or unworthy). Additionally, the authors argue that "models of others can be positive or negative (others are seen as available and caring, or as unreliable or rejecting)."[19]

Below you will find two loose interpretations of the Four Category Model:

Positive Model of Others

	Secure	Preoccupied	
	"I will be safe"	"I will be safe if I keep you close"	
Negative Model of Self	*Dismissive*	*Fearful*	*Positive Model of Self*
	I will be safe if I keep you far from me because you might go	I will be safe if I push you away because I want you to stay	

Positive Model of Others

Figure 1. The Four Category Model diagramed in Henderson, Antonia, Kim Bartholomew, Shanna Trinke, and Marilyn Kwong. "When Loving Means Hurting: An Exploration of Attachment and Intimate Abuse In a Community Sample." *Journal of Family Violence* 20 (August 1, 2005): 220, fig. 1.

Secure	**Preoccupied**
—Emotionally Safe; Feeling Secure in connection; When conflict arises there is a positive sense of resolution	—Feelings of anxiety in the relationship may occupy thoughts and ways to stay close; worrying about emotional distance in the relationship; fear of desertion
Dismissing	**Fearful**
Described as overly independent; not needy in the relationship; pride in emotional autonomy within the relationship	—Desires closeness in the relationship but is fearfully cautious to seek it due to feelings of unworthiness —Fearing the absolution of the relationship at any moment

Figure 2. The Four Category Model as described in

Feeney, Judith A. "Adult Romantic Attachment: Developments in the Study of Couple Relationships." In *Handbook of Attachment: Theory, Research, and Clinical Applications*, edited by Jude Cassidy and Phillip R. Shaver, Third edition. (New York: The Guilford Press, 2016): 439, fig. 2.1.

Individuals who are *securely attached* see themselves as confident in their ability to access their primary attachment figure during moments of perceived external threats. They experience low attachment anxiety, and this is evident in the way they engage their partners. They see themselves as worthy of love and their loved one as available and accepting. Their behaviors within the relationship are reflective of this sense of emotional safety and security.

Preoccupied or anxiously attached individuals experience a high level of self-doubt and confidence in their worthiness to be loved and attended to. However, they have a positive regard and view of others, which leads to being overly dependent upon their partner for feelings of worth and security.

The *dismissive-avoidant* type has high positive regard for self and independence within relationships. However, they have a negative view of being able to access love, attention, and reliable care because they fear rejection during times of perceived external threat.

Lastly, *fearful-avoidant* individuals experience both high attachment anxiety and a negative view of self and others. They long for attachment and closeness and simultaneously fear it. They will, of course, want love and affection, but they may also avoid them by maintaining emotional distance in order to protect against the overwhelming fear of rejection.

While there is much research on how early childhood trauma can affect attachment and bonding throughout the lifespan, this does not negate the impact of trauma occurring in later stages of adolescent and adult development. In fact, relational trauma occurring at any point in the lifespan may create maladjustments in the quality of an individual's relational attachment engagements. To the degree an individual perceives having experienced a significant and sudden rip in the bonding construct one possesses within, pathways to connection are reorganized with what may seem to be indelible prints. However, these imprints are not necessarily permanent.

When a close relationship has experienced meaningful conflict surrounding issues such as loss, financial hardship, betrayal, etc., the relationship and the individuals comprising it may experience a disruption in the primary attachment system. In other words, the individual may experience a series of changes in their ability to engage in the relationship securely. This may also affect their sense of being able to obtain emotional safety and security within their most important relationships as well as the sense of self-worthiness of being able to receive it.

If this is you, you might have noticed some profound changes in your behaviors, thoughts, and emotions during moments of distress in your marriage. For instance, in your marriage, you may have enjoyed open communication. When there were communication challenges, you addressed them with your partner. Sure, there were the common disagreements within the marriage, but you always knew that distress was momentary and could be resolved eventually. Your partner was your best friend and, because of that, you talked about almost anything. You enjoyed spending time with one another and not just doing activities. When you were at home doing nothing, there was enjoyment and peace. When there were issues at work or elsewhere, you knew your partner would be there. In fact, of all the challenges that could and had arisen in your marriage, one thing you knew for sure was that undoubtedly you would always be there for one another.

Then the day came when you discovered the affair and all that you knew without doubt now came with suspicion. In this space, you find yourself more easily distressed within the relationship. Your ability to express your needs and maintain feelings of closeness and intimacy have dramatically changed within the marriage. Now you may avoid closeness or constantly worry about it. You might even wonder if you are worthy of being loved the way you had hoped. Though you want and long for this connection, it now seems elusive. In all the ruminating, you ask yourself, *Will it ever be the same again?* This is not uncommon. In fact, many individuals like you desire and seek to restore and re-pattern the quality of attachment and bonding engagement in the relationship.

The important thing to know here is that such desires may be addressed within the context of a relationship.

This can be seen in the case of our couple who were still actively assessing the impact to the marriage after the affair through marriage counseling. They had elected to undergo the process of assessing and working toward eventual integration of what they have described as an uncharacteristic preoccupation and anxiety about closeness to one another in the marriage. Their hope in doing so is that their innate wiring and disposition for closeness and interdependence within the marriage will return them to the relationship they once enjoyed. They wanted to return to the place where they knew that no matter the hurdle, they would be there for one another, accepting each other, that no matter the challenge, they could do almost anything as long as they did so together. Their love would belong to one another.

Writing Prompt

Take some time to loosely assess what patterns you most likely identify with. Review the text above in order to find patterns that closely resemble the ways you adapt to moments of relational disconnection. The purpose here is not to diagnose but rather to provide context to the ways you may respond to the loss of connection in your relationship so that you can fully understand the possible origins of behaviors and emotions when engaging your partner. This will help you to monitor your responses to relational distress and, more importantly, assist you to move toward behaviors that more specifically reflect your desires for closeness.

CHAPTER 5

COMMUNICATION

What do you do when you want to speak but the words inside of you aren't words yet? They are feelings, and because there are so many, you find yourself grasping at the next nearest words you can muster during conversation with your partner. In doing so, the conversation can sometimes be riddled with questions when you want to make a statement and periods when you are seeking to find an answer. It seems obvious to you that your partner would know the message you are trying to communicate, and this adds to the hurt when the meaning is not received. Instead of sharing, it seems as though the conversation turns into an argument. In your heart, you are hoping your partner will see your need and accept this. Instead, it seems as though you are met with defensiveness and then an attack. Each time you hope it will be different, but every time it seems the same. Eventually you're talking, but true communication is happening less and less frequently. If words were meat for consumption, you would find meager nourishment in the value of each morsel. Things are being said, but in truth, the heart of your thoughts are going increasingly unspoken.

When this happens, couples can find it difficult to even speak about daily, mundane tasks. Suddenly conversations about dishes can become an argument of highest proportion. Now that we know how attachment needs and the perception of threat can affect the quality of relational engagement, it stands to reason that this would also include components of communication.

Communication is an important tool in the remedy of affair recovery. If there were an anecdote or medicinal remedy for the affliction of infidelity and betrayal, communication in its varying forms would be a very necessary binder for the main ingredients. It helps to bond the multiple skills that are helpful in the process of relational repair. This is the process of recovery, and communication is the mainstay in treatment. That being said, there is quite a bit of helpful information on communication and how to communicate in multiple environments.

For our purposes, we will cover several core parts that I have found to be foundational in beginning to have honest, transparent, and vulnerable conversations. This may be difficult for you. You may already be asking how this is possible when there is a tremendous degree of mistrust in the marriage. Or, as the injured party, you may question the purpose of communicating transparently and openly when your partner has betrayed your trust.

For those who have been unfaithful in the marriage, you too will question the goal in vulnerable communication when it seems like your partner is simply looking to rehash painful wounds and that, no matter what you say, they will not believe you. For you, it will seem that each conversation is an opportunity to attack. Communication will seem like a battleground where your spouse's weapons of warfare will seem formidable and shrewd. Every conversation for you will come with a risk of veering away from hope on the horizon and ending up in the land of painful words where they always abide. That's where the place of pain is remembered, and so you will do your best to avoid this compounding calamity with many strategies. Ultimately, however, the reality is that no strategies will do as well as simply having healthy communication with your partner.

This was quite evident in the relationship between Rebecca and Kevin. Kevin described a really bad argument that once occurred between him and Rebecca. It started when Rebecca mentioned going on a family vacation during the summer. Rebecca was discussing activities for the family like they always had done. Each year they would pack the family up and head to a new destination to discover different parts of the US. Sometimes they would fly, and sometimes they would drive. No matter the route, this had become part of family tradition, but it was one that had begun to slip after the affair. Like clockwork, they would discuss plans for the upcoming summer well in advance in order to plan and solidify trip details. Rebecca thought it would be a great reminder of something enjoyable they could both discuss, even though they were a bit behind this year. To Rebecca, it did not matter. The purpose in bringing up the conversation was not necessarily to plan the trip during a conversation while riding in the vehicle, but rather, in her mind, a momentary idea that brought a smile to her face, and one she believed would be a nice reprieve from everything else going on in the marriage.

However, the conversation did not resonate for Kevin in the same way. Though Kevin did enjoy the family trips as much as Rebecca, the timing had a new meaning to him. You see, they always traveled as a family the week after the 4th of July. They always found the best rates after the holiday and could buy a lot of the incidentals at low cost because of the post-holiday sales. In fact, both of them almost enjoyed planning for the trip and saving money for it with their combined strategies and goals for this time of the year as much as they did going on the actual trip. However, this time of the year that also now reminded Kevin of the affair. This was now The Affair Anniversary.

Kevin learned of the affair one night while checking the home office computer for recent plans the couple had made for an upcoming trip. The device that they both used for phone calls was a shared system, one which happened to back up files and messaging onto their computer. It was there that he found messages, pictures, and other files. That was the moment everything changed. For Kevin, the moment is its own event, complete with ritual, tradition, and negative memories. When that day comes to mind, Kevin finds himself checking on things in the marriage, ruminating on what he was thinking and feeling during that moment, and vividly envisioning all the details that led to the revelation of the affair. When this happens, all of the emotions rush in and it is like being transported back to the day of discovery.

So when Rebecca mentioned the annual family trip and planning for it, Kevin was reminded of the time he had discovered the affair while planning the family trip. The idea of planning reminded him of that time last year when his whole world had changed. What happened afterward became an argument that led to a brief separation for the couple. Rebecca decided she would do her best to avoid that ever happening again. They both learned here that any communication in their marriage was a possible terrain of rocky ground and pitfalls that could lead to emotionally dangerous places.

In addressing this, both were initially given a few tools to restart and calibrate conversations between one another. This included the daily mundane topics and those pertaining specifically to the affair. I wanted Rebecca and Kevin to know that they had the tools to confidently support one another during difficult conversations and to also know they had tools to express their desires in ways that helped their partner to hear and meet their needs. This would be a foundational instrument for initial discussion but, more importantly, a necessary mechanism for helping to heal wounds and reconcile parts of the marriage that had been divided.

In the next section, we will identify and add several tools for repairing, developing, and strengthening communication within your marriage.

Many of the communication strategies we will discuss are adapted from an intervention used in a particular method of clinical couples counseling. This intervention originates from a methodology called Imago Therapy, which is a methodology for couples counseling and a model for understanding and treating partner relationships. While we will not study in great detail all the tenets pertaining to this methodology, it is important to know the framework from which we will pull the collection of tools used during an intervention called *Intentional Dialogue*. Before we describe this intervention, let's briefly discuss Imago Therapy as best interpreted from a broad viewpoint.

Imago Therapy was founded by Dr. Harville Hendrix and Dr. Helen La-Kelly Hunt in 1980.[20] The term *imago* is Latin for the word *image*. The idea is that we subconsciously choose partners who represent the picture or image of someone who has the capacity help us heal from early childhood wounds and thus be made whole. Our subconscious leans toward healing and is seeking to work through early traumas in order to "restore aliveness and wholeness" through the use of subconsciously selected proxies who most closely remind us of the dynamic between our childhood version of self in relationship to our caregiver.[21] This subconscious pairing subsequently triggers familiar patterns and interactions that originated from our primitive parts of our brain and have now adapted in our partner relationships. The key is that the originating primitive thoughts, feelings, and behaviors serve a familiar function in current romantic relationships. Once you can uncover the longings and desires behind the originating primitive reactions, then you are bringing the subconscious to the conscious and are now able to help one another work through previously painful unmet needs and heal together.

One of the principal interventions used in Imago is the Imago Dialogue. This dialogue technique is a clinical intervention used in the process to help partners "restructure the way you talk to each other, so that what you say to each other is mirrored back to you, is validated, and empathized with."[22] You can use the Imago Dialogue to tell each other all about your childhoods, to state your frustrations clearly, and to articulate exactly what you need from each other in order to heal. While this structured intervention is best used as a component in the overall approach to Imago Therapy, we will be pulling aspects of this intervention in order to use its most helpful tenets for complex and affair-related conversations. For a complete approach to this intervention and within its framework, you will want to seek out a professional clinical mental health counselor for further assistance and recommended guidance.

Let's briefly review the loosely adapted key components as written and discussed more in *Getting the Love You Want: A Couples Guide* by Dr. Harville Hendrix.[23]

Intentional Dialogue Review

Sender's Role

Make an Appointment

Schedule an agreed-upon time to communicate with your partner about a specific topic. When you are scheduling the appointment, ensure it is a time that both of you can agree to speak to one another without distraction. It will need to be a time where you both have time and emotional space to be able to discuss the important topic without rushing. This time may not actually be the time you approach your partner with your request to speak, but it should be timely. In fact, this time to communicate should commence at any point between the moment of inquiry and twenty-four hours later. This is very important. Too much time after the request to speak can create more resentment and confusion. Too little time after inquiry can create an opportunity where one partner may be experiencing heightened fight-or-flight arousal and may engage in the conversation with increased reactivity to triggers. Schedule a time where each of you know that negative activations will be low and either neutral or positive emotional presence is high in order to properly engage one another in a time of sensitive need.

Declare a Statement of Intention

Share the purpose in scheduling a time to communicate with your partner. Your intention is not to tell your partner how you feel so that they will comply with your demands and ultimately see the superiority of your perspective. On the contrary, it is your intention to invite your partner to a deeper space or deeper part of your world by sharing your deeply held thoughts and feelings because of the position your partner holds in your life. You are partnered, paired, and attached to one another in a way that most others outside of this sphere are unable to access. When you share your intention in communicating with your partner, you are essentially saying, "You are of prime importance to me. Because of how dearly I value you in my life, I desire to know and be known by you." Though you may not explicitly use these words to invite your partner into a discussion, your invitation should nonetheless reflect this motivating feature in wanting to intimately communicate with your partner. Instead of saying, "We need to talk," try saying instead, "I value our relationship and because of this, I am hoping that if we can revisit this issue, it will only add worth to both you and I together." Of course, use your own words, but the point here is that your intention to communicate with one another is the motivation that undergirds the reason you are even together. Hold on to this and be able to communicate this when attempting to express your desire in speaking to your partner.

Practice Pausing

Pause every three to four sentences to allow your partner to process the information being shared. Reflect on any meeting, class, or training you have attended where you found yourself mentally focusing in and out of the material information. Why is that? There can be many reasons and variables contingent upon the topic, time of day, individual wellness, and more. Often it may simply be the sheer volume of data being presented at one time. The issue is not how much you share, but rather how much you share in each moment. The message shared should be sent in ways that help your partner to hear the heart of your message. Like clues to an undiscovered treasure in a forest, each time you pause, you should leave a clear crumb, a clue to the treasure, the heart in your message. When you send a message, it is not enough to simply just verbalize the content; instead, it is your responsibility to do so in a way that assists the receiver in organizing the information in ways they can hear and receive it. Pausing every three to four sentences will help your partner to do just that.

Stay Specific

Select one topic to discuss during your time to communicate. Ensure that what you are discussing contains all of the details and specifics about the incident. However, avoid the pitfalls of aggregating the issue with all the other previous and similar issues to justify your point. When you do, it is as if you've taken all your message "breadcrumbs" and thrown them at your partner just before motioning for them to come and get you in the proverbial game of hide-and-seek. Remember that when sending a message, it is important to leave as many markers in the conversation as possible—the more specific, the better. In fact, here you can give as many details as you need, although only about the one specific issue. Imagine, for example, that you will be going to purchase a vehicle. In your planning you may consider the color, make, model, supplier, purchasing price, mileage, safety, resale value, and more. In all your planning, you would not also bring into discussion clothes. Clothes? Clothes have nothing to do with the intent to purchase a vehicle. Sure, you may look nice in certain vehicles wearing varying types of attire, but that may be its only relevance, and it certainly does not contribute to the overall intention to discuss, plan, and purchase a new vehicle. Yet this is what we do every time we attempt to associate non-essential details with the essential. Plan to discuss your topic with one issue in mind and then do so with as much corroborating information as possible, information pertaining to the one issue only. A great way to help you do this is by starting or orienting your sentence with a date and time. Use words and phrases like *yesterday, this morning, last night*, or *last month*, for example.

Use "I" Statements

Start your sentence with "I feel . . ." statements. When you speak to your partner, you want to do so in a way that takes ownership of your thoughts, feelings, and actions. Beginning your sentence with "I" will help you to do just that. However, what often happens is that we begin our statement with "I" and quickly follow it with "you." Take, for instance, "I feel you do not understand" or "I feel that you only care about you." There are a couple of problems with these statements even though they start with the word "I." The main problem is that while the aforementioned sentence starts with "I," it immediately shifts to "you," and no matter what is said afterwards, this risks blaming your partner instead of sharing with your partner, which is ultimately one of the main mechanisms toward resolve. First, when you start your sentence with "I" and then follow up with "feel," there should actually be a feeling word after the word *feel*. What often happens is that we stay cognitive and completely miss the emotion in the thought. The more you are able to express the emotion along with the thought, the better able your partner is able to find those "breadcrumb clues," as noted in our previous example. Using "I feel" with an actual feeling helps bring your partner into that deeply held inner emotional world. Not only will they be able to comprehend you better, but they will be able to hear you, which is what we all want in a relationship. Second, when you share your feelings, it is best to do so with very primary emotions.

Allow me to explain. There are primary and secondary emotions. Secondary emotions are resulting feelings from directly correlated emotions. Secondary emotions are those feelings that rise to the surface. They are your safe emotions. The ones that require the least amount of risk in displaying or sharing because they cover the most vulnerable of emotions. Secondary emotions are the most accessible. In fact, almost anyone may hear secondary emotions being shared in conversations almost anywhere and with almost anyone. These words may include *frustration, irritation, annoyance, satisfied*, and others. These are the emotions you see when you cut the line while in traffic and the driver next to you now yells with very animated lips message that would be incoherent were it not for the nonverbal hand gesturing toward you. They are the initial emotions you display in front of your spouse when you are in an argument. It is when you tell them how frustrated and disappointed you are in their actions, when deep down you actually feel sadness. This brings us to the next category of emotions: primary emotions. Primary emotions are the direct, unfiltered emotions that underlie often surfacing, secondary feelings. Primary emotions undergird the truest emotional intentions. According to the American Psychological Association dictionary, they are our basic core emotions, and they are universally recognized.[24] This means they generally require little social deconstruction; across social, culture, and generational variables, basic feelings such as sadness, fear, and joy are broadly recognized and persist. This is incredibly important to know when communicating emotions to your spouse. The communication path of least resistance is best journeyed with "I feel . . ." and a basic core emotion in order to increase understanding and receipt of your message, which can successfully cut across individual context differences you each bring to the relationship. In other words, while it may be tempting and more comfortable to share with your partner that you are annoyed with and disappointed in them, you risk sending a message that your partner will not fully understand and conceptualize the way in which you intended. It is not that those words are wrong to use, but rather that they increase the potential for sending a mixed message where the core need is unheeded and more importantly unmet. However, when you add disappointment and annoyance to your fear and sadness, suddenly the message becomes a lot louder, more concise, and a lot clearer. It is as if you have decoded the message in such a way that helps your partner to hear what was once a mystery but is now a precise signal, prompting a loving response to your relational distress. Next time you are in conflict with your partner, try adding elemental primary emotions to your secondary emotions as well.

Take Turns

There will be one role provider at a time. When you are engaged with another person during a difficult conflict, it can be more challenging to do so without specific expectations. In light of this, many spouses may find themselves in a competition to share their grievances in what can sometimes resemble a fight to a perceived finish line to relieve emotional distress. This fight can sometimes look like an all-out, no-holds-barred argument championship where no rules apply. It is in this space that some of the most damage can be inflicted on the marriage and can have lasting effects. In order to defuse the intensity of conflict during distressing arguments in the marriage and simultaneously increase the potential for resolving issues, it is important to establish and uphold standards of engaging one another during stressful conversations. One way to do this is by allowing one another to either send or receive a message when determining who will assume which role in the process of communicating with one another. If you share a message or a concern with your partner, you will be the only one to do so until you have fully explained your thoughts and emotions as described above. If you are receiving your spouse's message, you will fully assume this role without explaining, formulating, and/or ruminating on your position. If you are receiving, you will be like an empty vessel preparing to be filled with all the contents your partner is sharing with you at the moment. If you are full of your own story, you will overfill, and it will be nearly impossible to accept space for your spouse when they are sending a message. Equally the sender will know they are finished when their message in the proverbial bottle has been emptied. At this juncture, then and only then will you both want to trade roles in order to begin the process of sending and sharing a message.

Receiver's Role

Mirror Back

Reflect back what the other person is communicating. In mirroring, you exhibit back what your partner has shared with or presented to you. This can be verbal, nonverbal, or both. You want to imagine yourself as a literal mirror where you are imaging back gestures, intonation, posture, tone, cadence, volume, and of course the words themselves. You demonstrate this by beginning your sentence with "What I am hearing you say is . . ." Afterward, your sentence will end with "Tell me more." This exchange will move back and forth from sender to receiver until the sender communicates that there is nothing else to send. Some may find this initially a bit disingenuous. You may wonder if mirroring may look more like emotionless copying. However, just the opposite often occurs. In fact, it is this specific type of tracking that not only helps your partner to stay in step with the message you are sharing, but it is also how you will also know that your partner is right there with you. Hearing your partner reflect back your emotions, your thoughts, and the way in which you articulate them with brevity sends signals to your brain that your partner is present and in pursuit of you. The closer you mirror one another, the stronger the signal is to each other. It will be tempting to interpret and translate your spouse's expressions, but I caution you to be the mirror. Though you know your partner well and will undoubtedly succeed in understanding their message, it is equally important to do so in a way that sends the signal to them that you do indeed understand what they are trying to communicate. When you mirror your partner, you maximize the potential of doing just that. Your partner will have risked vulnerability to share a deeply held message, one which they now know for sure that you have received and heard. Once this can be established, almost anything can begin from this point. One word of caution about mirroring: you will certainly not want mirror highly escalated communication, as this intervention works efficiently and can magnify intense emotions despite the desired outcome. You will want to only mirror your partner when both of you can be assured of de-escalated emotions and having down-regulated activation of the human arousal response to emotional threat and safety.

Provide Validation

Confirm the worth of your partner's message. Validation affirms your partner's importance in having a platform to even share their concerns with you. Being allowed to bring their heartfelt concerns to you knowing that you care, knowing that you are accessible to their unmet needs and that you are understanding of their concerns, is incredibly validating to your partner. When you validate your partner's concerns, you are in essence communicating to your partner that you understand them, and that while others may consider their concerns illogical, you value them. At this point, you may be wondering whether validation communicates agreement when you may not agree with your spouse's concerns. To be clear, validation does neither. It cuts to the real heart of the issue, which is not agreement or compliance with any one perspective; instead, it satisfies the question of "got-ness" when the question is "Do you get me?" or "Can you see me?" When you validate your partner, the answer is a resounding *yes*. You can do this in dialogue when you begin your sentence with, "You make sense to me because . . ."

Empathy

Merriam-Webster's Dictionary defines "empathy" as vicariously experiencing thoughts, feelings, and experiences of another.[26] Empathy is so important that I have devoted a full section on this topic in the next chapter. Empathy can help soothe human arousal during the fight-or-flight response we experience when perceiving impending threat or danger. Empathy communicates proximity to your loved one and assures them that they are not alone. When you convey empathy to your partner, you do all of these things. The challenge, however, is in accurately conveying empathy. It is, for instance, our natural tendency to view others through ourselves. This self-orienting point of view can hinder us from vicariously experiencing others' views. We may say things such as "If I were you," but what we often mean is "If I were you but still being me." Empathy causes us to imagine momentarily a world where "If I were you simply as you." When we vicariously convert to their perspective, then we can directly convey with honest emotion the feelings that we feel with our partner. When this happens, you hold this vulnerable space together. You increase feelings of closeness, proximity, and connection. You can do this by simply beginning your sentence with "I can imagine feeling . . ." When you do this, make sure to include all of the secondary and primary emotions in order to fully express empathy for your partner during times of emotional distress. Remember the vulnerable core emotions and the extended second layer emotions are often the keys to being able to more closely empathize with your partner.

Writing Prompt

Apply these strategies in part or in whole as a way to manage and restart conversations around difficult topics. These tools are best used in concert with a clinical therapist for coaching in effectively using the whole intervention, during both times of distress and moments of encouragement within the relationship. Whether you use these strategies or others, make sure you have effectively established a framework through which both you and your spouse will effectively tackle tough conversations during moments of relational conflict.

CHAPTER 6

EMPATHY

It was around the sixth and seventh session that Kevin began to really process the underlying motivations behind his triggers. Kevin shared an example once where he had asked Rebecca about an incident where she had called home early in the afternoon and stated that she would be home late due to a last-minute project with her team. Kevin was familiar with Rebecca's career and the type of work required to accomplish certain assignments, so for him it was nothing out of the ordinary. He did not like her having to work so late at times and had talked to her about the possibility of changing companies, as he recognized she enjoyed the work she did and was good at it. However, she frequently complained about the workload distribution and scheduled hours. He did not like seeing her exhausted and wanted to help her find a way to resolve this issue. However, it was her decision and, though he did not like it, he was willing to support her and the family where he could when her work projects consumed more of her personal time than desired. That night, however, he got a call from her that seemed no different than the others until he found out about the affair, and it became clear that this night had not been like the other times. This particular evening, Rebecca had been in another city with her affair partner. They were out of town for a work project that day and had planned to return at the end of the workday but ended up staying later. She and the affair partner had ended up getting a hotel and having sex.

This was a night that Kevin would ask Rebecca about deeply explicit details. He wanted to know how she felt when she was having sex with the other man. He wanted to know what she was thinking when they were having sex.

He also wanted to know what she was wearing, what she said to the affair partner, if she enjoyed being with him, and if she ever thought of Kevin. The interesting thing is that Kevin had asked these questions a number of times. The questions would come up periodically and seemingly at random. They would come up before bedtime, when they were driving in the car, after dinner, when they spoke on the phone, in the morning before work, even when they were sharing a joke, until there was nothing funny. The questions were sometimes worded the same and other times with different inflection points, but the answer never satisfied his deeper need to know. That was because prior to counseling, Kevin had not known the true question. Sure, Rebecca would answer the questions, quickly but not easily. She, of course, feared the answers would cause more harm than good. However, she did dutifully answer, pushing back her own negative emotions and fears about the impending threat to their marriage with each repetitive answer. The issue, however, for Kevin and Rebecca was that though the questions were being asked and answered, they really were not the true questions.

You see, Kevin initially thought that having an answer for each question at any time would show him that Rebecca was being truthful, and it would quell the nervousness and fear about the relationship when those emotions stirred inside of him. It rarely did. When it did, it did not last, and those resurfacing insecurities would prompt more questions for more answers. Kevin had to realize that there was a deeper question, a deeper need, and a deeper longing that needed to be satisfied. He realized during sessions that it was from this place that almost all of his questions originated. It was the absence of this knowledge that initially contributed to what at times became an insatiable desire to know and know again the answer to all these questions. It was only when Kevin discovered that what he really sought to know was that she truly still loved him and that she valued him. He wanted to know that he was valuable and worthy to his wife. When he asked what she thought of him when she was with the affair partner, he really wanted to know if she thought he was still worthy. When he wondered what she was wearing or thinking about or whether she would adorn herself especially for the affair partner, what he truly wanted to know was if he was somewhere in her mind, because then he would know that he was still valued by her and thus worthy to her. Kevin longed to know this, and almost every question he asked was some facet of this deeper question he carried. In almost every conversation pertaining to the affair and the message he truly needed to send, it was instead the meta messages that he sent out, hoping it would return with the core answer. Kevin would eventually come to know the question and recognize when he had an answer. It was the answer by way of empathy that would allow him to receive what felt like a balm to an unreachable internal wound. It took the work of knowing what Kevin needed in order to quench the emotional thirst that yearned within, and it was Rebecca's job to be able to hear, hold, and heal with Kevin with each attempt he made in vulnerably sharing what his true needs were in the moment.

Allow me to explain. Frequently, it is not the absence of data, ideas, or solutions in our attempts to resolve conflict within our marriages that is the issue; in reality, the barrier to resolution often lies in knowing that our partner can vicariously know, understand, and feel what we are feeling. When we are unsure about whether our partner can know, understand, and feel what we are feeling—because they are our person and it is our desire to know and be known by them—then we can often find ourselves continuously explaining and behaving in ways that seek to help our partner know what we know and feel what feel. It is not that they will have full knowledge of your personal and direct experience; it is instead that they will be able to envision your emotional experience more clearly because now they know the motivating desire of your deepest need. And in sharing from this place, your partner will also now be better able to journey with you to understanding and healing.

It is in the emotional journey together that empathy abounds. There is no shorter path to the destination of healing and few other vehicles to use than that of empathy. It is more than saying "I understand" to your partner. It is more than saying "I am sorry." It happens each time you hear one another when sharing. It happens when either literally you are holding one another or conveying this sentiment when you simply remain wholly emotionally present while sharing. It can also happen whenever you can successfully heal a piece of the relationship together, because when you do so now, you are connecting empathically with one another. Sharing empathy will allow the injured partner to take part in helping the injurer to heal individually. I have found no greater ingredient in the process of mending a marriage injured by infidelity than that of the power of empathy.

Writing Prompt

Take a moment to determine and write down ways in which you have been able to hear your partner's emotional experience recently. Ensure that you have held or examine how you will hold emotional space with your partner's experience, either by checking in with one another for emotional understanding or by scheduling time to express vulnerable emotions. Lastly, jot down times when both you and your partner were able to heal even a small piece of the relationship as a tool for reflection.

CHAPTER 7

INTIMACY

It had been several months since Kevin had even touched Rebecca, as Rebecca explained during one of our sessions. Though she and Kevin were in counseling and had decided to work on their marriage, she wondered if he still desired her and found her attractive. Though she recognized the irony of the one who had had an extramarital affair wondering whether her partner found her attractive, for her there was never a time she did not want Kevin or found him undesirable. We would later continue to work through processing her deep fears within the relationship as well as unhealthy thought patterns pertaining to the lead-up of the affair. However, for Rebecca, intimacy had always been an affirming and validating act of belonging and love between her and Kevin. Having that part of their relationship become so fragile and intermittent, especially in moments of distress, added to Rebecca's feelings of loneliness and her fear of rejection.

Kevin, on the other hand, was riddled with questions about what he called Rebecca's propensity for disloyalty. For him, it wasn't just that she cheated, but it was the number of lies that went into the entire affair. There had been moments that Kevin had suspected the possibility of his partner having an affair before it all came to light. However, she had always had a response to explain away his suspicions. Kevin recalled a time when he asked her face-to-face and, without missing a beat, Rebecca had always had an answer.

As much as Kevin had enjoyed the sexual relationship he had had with his wife and still desired to be with her physically, there were moments where the pain of betrayal was much greater than the longing for sexual intimacy and desire. This added to the emotional distance that both felt in their marriage. While they both wanted to feel the closeness they had once enjoyed in their marriage, they too felt the chasm of space in their intimacy within the marriage. It would be their efforts to increase proximity in their relationship that would help to revive intimacy once again.

There are a few ways you can pursue intimacy as a strategy to help repair your marriage after an affair.

As described in Chapter 4, a young child is able to feel most secure and confident in their relationship and their ability to explore the world around them when there is this sense of having a *secure base*.[27] Knowing that only a short distance away there is a safe, secure, and accessible caregiver provides the certainty that they need in their ability to then venture away. This dynamic occurs as a function in the attachment-seeking principle of proximity, which plays in the hardwiring from our earliest bonding experiences. It is proximity to a loving caregiver from an attachment theory perspective that helps to explain our drive and utilized mechanisms for bonding and connection.

Sue Johnson, founder of Emotionally Focused Therapy, once said that "sex is an activity of bonding."[28] If attachment and connection were a beautiful tapestry, woven within the fabric are bonded fibers. However, they are stitched together by proximity. This principle of proximity helps to make the beautiful relationship quilt. It is a core component of empathy as well as intimacy. In order to experience intimacy with another person, you have to get close. In order to be intimate with your spouse, you will need to do even more. Intimacy requires decreasing the space between you and the other. It means decreasing the physical or emotional distance between you and your spouse.

Although for some, having more sex may be the goal in reading through this chapter, I assure you that there is no better ingredient to having a healthy sexual relationship than having more intimacy. This can be thought of in several different categories. They are in no particular order, and they are best thought of as a holistic approach to achieving greater intimacy. However, improvement in one or more categories will also enhance your ability to both experience and cultivate intimacy with your spouse.

1. *Intimate Emotional Proximity*—It is crucial to feel what the other feels. Emotional proximity means being able to, in part, feel the feelings your

partner possesses. It is only in part, of course, because you are a separate human being, complete with your own uniqueness, so this hinders to some degree your ability to fully assume the emotional experiences of your partner. Simply put, you are not your spouse. You are a separate individual. However, the thing that separates you can also connect you in that each of you are human beings. The emotional palette is an experience common to humankind. While you may not have experienced the specific emotion of your spouse in this particular moment, complete with their own particular experiences, you have most likely experienced their core emotions, which we know are common to all of mankind. Whether you are articulate in expressing your emotions or not, remember that you have felt core emotions such as sadness, joy, and fear, because core primary emotions are universal. Knowing this allows you to pursue emotional intimacy even in the darkest of spaces. It is the vicarious emotional experience of your partner's feelings that will be the light. When you are seeking to increase intimate emotional intimacy with each other, you create opportunities to sit with one another's emotional experience within the relationship or when you share your core emotions with your partner in a moment of vulnerability. Maybe it happens when you simply listen for your partner's emotional needs when the message coming out is cognitive. Perhaps it will be in the early morning hours when you read from a journal entry you've written about the marriage or when you've just completed a letter of all the things you hope for in your marriage. Yes, there will be many opportunities and many opportunities to miss. Intimate emotional proximity will not happen automatically, especially when there has been an injury to the relationship bond. It will feel scary and dangerous, and to be honest, it will be. There will be no guarantees diving into the ocean of emotions with yourself and together. You will not have to dive deep every time, however, in order to obtain the spoils of the wreckage. Sometimes what you are both looking for emotionally in the relationship will be right on the surface. It will require knowing that you both are on a fascinating journey of discovering things about one another together. In the end, what you are building will not be the same. It may be different, but it can be good too.

2. *Intimate Physical Proximity*—Be close in the spatial sense. Intimate physical proximity means to be next to. Instead of leaving the room, you stay. Instead of stepping away, you step toward. Instead of walling yourself off, you keep the wall down. It is decreasing the physical space between you and your partner. There are of course people who have differing com-

fort levels of physical contact, and this is not necessarily synonymous to intimate physical proximity. To be clear, decreasing physical proximity is certainly a by-product of increasing physical contact. However, increasing physical proximity does not necessarily include touch. Physical proximity means to occupy physical space with your partner. For some partners, it may be too distressing to engage in physical contact too early in the healing process of the marriage. Physical touch may be a trigger and could lead to increasing conflict within the marriage. However, because we are social beings and wired for connection and closeness, as discussed in earlier chapters, we know that physical closeness is an important component of building connection and intimacy within a relationship. So how do you decrease physical proximity between you and your partner or, to phrase it differently, increase physical closeness? You do it by being physically near, especially during times of emotional distress where possible in the relationship. Just being there can be incredibly soothing for your partner in moments of conflict, whether you are touching one another or not. Being in the room, being in the car, being on the couch, being on the porch, being in the bed, and yes, being in each other's arms are just some of the ways in which you can develop and restore physical intimacy within the marriage. Sometimes intimate physical proximity will lead to touch. The key is to know presence and proximity can happen on a continuum of physicality, and how this may look different in application from marriage to marriage. There is, in my view, one indisputable notion in this matter of repairing intimacy: whether you are touching one another or not, you must know that you are both there.

3. *Intimate Cognitive Proximity*—Work to understand the thoughts of your partner. Intimate cognitive proximity is more of an endeavor. It is the work of learning to understand as accurately as possible how your partner processes a matter. This can be a tough one because, for some, this may be interpreted as agreeing with your partner's thoughts on the matter. On the contrary, you may disagree with your partner's thoughts on an issue and inevitably still understand their thought position. It is understanding but also knowing their thoughts that leads to proximity. Quite literally, it is sharing your thoughts with one another that leads to this level of understanding and closeness. When you share with one another, you are able to understand your partner's personal thoughts. This sharing becomes an opportunity where within your partner's mind, there exists a place for intimate communion with you. This is a place where few are invited and you, being their most intimate loving relationship, possess

the key to this private location. The door is not easily found, however. It will take more than just holding a designated position in your partner's life and more than simply banging on the proverbial door. It will take a gentle, consistent knocking, and the entry of their deepest and most private thoughts will gain you access to the inner corridor of their mind. This gentle knocking will not be abstract; it will look like daily invitations for your partner's thoughts. It will look like you asking them to help you to know a particular matter pertaining to the marriage as they know it. It will look like you explaining your point of view on an issue with gentleness, thereby inviting them to share with you. It might also look like those moments after a disagreement when you schedule time to have *intentional dialogue*. There is no shortage of ways but instead a potential abundance of moments where you both can work to create an atmosphere in which each of you stay close to each other's private and intimate thoughts.

4. *Intimate Spiritual Proximity*—This involves drawing near to the inner essence of a romantic partner. Some will understand this as drawing close to their partner's spirit or the invisible energy of their spouse. Others may understand this as the core makeup of their partner's thoughts, feelings, personality traits, and so forth. However, you may better understand the terms *spirit* and *spirituality*, so the main takeaway is understanding that there is a part of your spouse that is not easily visible to the physical realm. It is a faith in knowing, though lacking physical evidence, that your partner is more than what your natural senses perceive. There is a centrally organized material to your partner that makes up who they are at their foundation. When you tap into this space, you find yourself really fellowshipping with the core of who your partner is and always will be. Intimate spiritual proximity is companionship at the deepest level. Acknowledging this part of your partner and seeking to decrease the distance here increases the closeness at a spiritual level. It is a relationship at the soul level. This is one of the deepest thresholds for intimacy. In order to do this, both partners will need to be open to understanding their own internal essence and being. It will mean seeing your personality and energy as a function of processes originating deep within your soul. Once you know this and can spend time with this knowledge, then you will be ready to share this with your partner. For some people this may take the shape of meditating together or praying together. Others will find that writing—or inscribing to some permanent artifact what your life mission and relationship goals are—is the avenue to cultivating intimate spiritual

proximity. It may even be worshiping together at your local church, synagogue, or other faith-based organization. Whichever task materializes and is implemented, your challenge will be in creating moments for attending to spiritual proximity in order to experience intimacy more fully within your marriage.

Writing Prompt:

Take some time to reflect on where you are in the marriage with respect to each dimension of intimacy within the marriage. Think of where your partner may be in this spectrum. Then discuss with one another the challenges and where in this spectrum you find yourself wanting to personally improve upon within the marriage.

This will not be the time to discuss what your partner is not doing right or where they have done wrong in contributing to the intimacy challenges within the marriage. Instead, this is an opportunity to reflect on your needs and determine where you could access those needs best as described through our four categories of improving intimacy within the marriage.

Once you have had this discussion with one another, determine what will be the best ways to intentionally and regularly reestablish and strengthen the intimacy within the marriage. Write down your thoughts to help facilitate deeper reflection. The more you fortify the bond of connection through closeness and intimate proximity, the more prepared you both will be to restore healthy love, from which outgrows more loving and bonding activities within your marriage.

CHAPTER 8

TRUST

Kevin and Rebecca both loved the water. They had a history of enjoying family vacations together and made it a point to be waterside whenever they could. Through the years, Kevin had discovered the art of sailing. During one session where he was describing his recreational time and things that he would do to manage stress, Kevin explained his understanding and fascination with boating. Specifically, Kevin enjoyed sailing. He said once that being out in the waters was a way for him to remove the pressures, and sometimes the weight of life's challenges, from his shoulders. He recognized that when life became overwhelming or felt too hurried that he could slow it down even if just for a few hours by simply spending time at the marina or out in the water or on his boat.

Kevin described a time when he and his family had encountered some rough waters. It was nothing he was too concerned about, as it was the remnants of a recent passing storm. It was a beautiful day, and he and his family had weathered challenging waves before. On their way in, he noticed that the wind speed indicator stopped functioning properly. He had the boat pointed in the direction that they wanted to go and could estimate from his experience and an internal knowledge of how fast the wind was that day. The boat was able to get a good jib through the waves though they were pushing into the boat downward. They angled northward and gathered speed with additional wind, allowing them open access to the sea and thus their intended destination. There had been nothing significant about this moment except that Kevin had marveled about his ability to helm a vessel. It was one of the places he felt the most confident. It was there that he could plot the course. With his instruments at his disposal, he could prepare the boat, anticipate with weather, and navigate potential rough waves with execution and strategy.

Sometimes he and his wife took the boat out with just the two of them. His wife would call him Captain Kevin at times. He laughed aloud with the title, as it was normally said during moments when Kevin would find himself explaining the process and the importance of safe sailing to his partner. Yes, he would laugh, but inside he admitted it made him smile. It made him feel assured of his role in the family and with his wife. He knew Rebecca trusted in him and, though he was the captain, he trusted in her too.

Trust is frequently assumed early on in a relationship. There may be parts of the relationship that require proving in order to gain full trust in the relationship with a new partner. However, in most marriages, two individuals come together assuming the best of one another.

When there is a betrayal of trust in the relationship, those two can grapple with now only seeing the worst. For some it will feel like living with the enemy, sleeping with the enemy, being married to the enemy, and yet loving the enemy. When your mind perceives your partner as the enemy, it may threaten your ability relax, feel safe, and let your guard down with your partner. The trust has been snatched away and, as hard as both partners try to search for what was initially a ubiquitous commodity, this valuable item seems nowhere to be found. Just when you think it is within reach, it disappears again. You think that you trust your partner, and then the phone rings and you wonder who they are talking to. You trust your spouse when they say that they are going to the store, but then the trip takes longer than you expect. You trust them to take a business trip because it has always been a part of their job duties, until the time comes for them to travel. You trust them to go spend time with their friends because recreation time with friends has always been important to the relationship, except the next time is tonight, and you did not expect tonight to come so soon. You trust your spouse until they ask you to trust.

Then you become hyperaware of your distrust. You want to trust your spouse again; if only removing this hyperawareness were that easy. Not only are you keenly aware of the distrust you have in the marriage and in your partner, but you may even question your ability to trust yourself. You wonder how you could have missed the signs. You may ask yourself how you could have so freely trusted your partner. You blame yourself. You ask, "Can I be trusted to know when to trust in my marriage again?" There is no easy way to satisfy this internal question.

However, there are a couple things that are known for sure: rebuilding trust will take repetition, intention, and duration. While trust initially in your relationship may have felt less formulaic and more organic, reestablishing trust will not be so. It will require several variables applied in a way that establishes the solution to the trust dilemma within your relationship. These three ingredients will be the foundation for redeveloping the trust framework of your marriage: repetition, intention, and duration. Better said, "But the key to trust is action, and, in particular commitment: commitments made and commitments honored."[29]

Trust Framework: Repetition, Intention, Duration

Repetition

According to Robert C. Solomon in *Building Trust: In Business, Politics, Relationships, and Life*, "Just as trust requires reinforcement, repetition, and new test and responsibilities, trust once betrayed remains open to new possibilities, new tests and new opportunities if only we will resolve, and commit ourselves to restore that trust."[30] Therefore, according to this perspective, Repetition is the reinforcements that trust requires for restoration. Repetition is quite literally repeating an action. Repetition is useful for learning a new skill or for establishing a new habit. It can be used to develop a level of mastery in a particular area. Sometimes it is used as an intervention for obtaining similar results after completing a specific set of actions.

Think of times when you have used repetition for a specific task. Ask yourself what the purpose was of applying repetition. Consider what the outcome was after demonstrating repetition. Now determine what the costs and gains in your repetition were. Maybe there were losses and that was a factor in your repetitive action. Lastly, consider applying this level of repetition to the area of trust in your marriage. You will need to assess the gains and the costs in your endeavor to consistently repeat trust-building actions in your marriage. Doing so will help you to commit to the routine of action. It will orient your reason for performing a behavior that seemingly should have yielded much earlier results. When your actions seem redundant, it will help you do it and then do it again because you understand the importance of repetition as a core component of the trust you so long to have again in your marriage.

Repetition in your marriage will include both the meaningful and mundane behaviors demonstrated regularly in the marriage. It is when you know that your spouse struggles with knowing what is on your agenda and you both develop a routine for sharing it. It can happen when your spouse asks for ways to be able to check in and you both have agreed upon a method for regularly doing so. It could be when your spouse asks to check your phone log and instead of allowing this to become another opportunity for distrust and contention, you both strategically use these moments for rebuilding trust by discussing consistent ways in which this information can be shared. Perhaps it is simply when either one of you asks to complete some chore of the day—such as picking up the car from the shop, finishing up the grocery list, or following up on a financial obligation—and instead of putting it off for later, you set it before you in the now in order to complete the behavior you were tasked with. This, too, shows consistency.

Although it may seem insignificant, integrity in small areas of daily life will strengthen the larger message of commitment toward repairing your relationship. This repetition demonstrates reliance, and it is another deposit in the well of trust.

Intention

Repetition is not random acts of behavior as a rule, nor will it be in the case of rebuilding trust in your marriage. Instead, it is best implemented with specific intentions. It is the intention behind your actions that will increase the probable outcome. It would be like assuming you will become a professional soccer player by occasionally hitting at a ball. Sure, you would have acquired some parallel skills; however, without specific purpose, they are unlikely to yield the intended results. It is the same in your marriage. In other words, your focus on specific ways in which you desire your marriage to heal will require your attention to tasks that are known and, when combined, assist with the rebuilding of trust.

The purposeful and intentional actions you take within in your marriage are a necessary key to affecting the goal you endeavor toward: rebuilding trust. Therefore, it will be important to understand the type of behavior implemented and the expected consequence of your action. For instance, if it is your desire that your spouse trusts you when you have to leave for business trips, determine and discuss with your spouse what specific actions you both could agree on. Discuss what would help ease your and your partner's fears and anxieties about you being away from home. You may decide that each of you will want to check in at the end of the night while away or that you will both talk about your agendas. Perhaps you both will simply talk about your emotional distress in navigating the fragility of your trust bond while you're away for travel. Whatever you both decide, determine what action can be taken regularly to help with the specific goal of rebuilding trust in the specific area of concern.

This means you will need to get narrow when you think of a behavior in response to distress experienced in the marriage from a trigger of distrust. Staying narrow, or focused, will help you stay more intentional. It will not be helpful enough to simply require that each of you trust one another. Instead, it will be your narrow scope of chosen actions, applied regularly for the purpose of easing points of distress in the marriage relative to trust.

Before you respond to conflict in this area of the marriage, think about what you want to convey by your actions. In this part of your marriage, your actions will speak just as loud as your words. The effort behind your actions will be just as loud in message as the action itself to your partner.

As the injured partner, you may find the display of your partner's consistent effort in demonstrating examples of their reliability in this area of the marriage toward you to be a visible sign that they want to cultivate a sense of safety and security within the relationship. All of this can happen when you are intentional with the actions and behaviors used as tools to create and rebuild the trust in your marriage.

Duration

" Trust like love, is an emotional skill, and ongoing dynamic, aspect of relationships."[31] Rebuilding trust will take time. There will be no quick way to get there. If trust were a highly desired destination for every traveler with quick wait times and limitless routes, everyone would get there. However, the reality is that, after an affair, this destination becomes more like a journey with long wait times and few routes. The good news is that once you arrive, you can stay as long as you like because you've now learned the route. Instead of relying on happenstance, accidents, bad directions, and memory, you and your partner have learned how to get where you are going in your goal of rebuilding trust. It will have taken you longer and it will seem as though at times you may be going in circles, but it will be this grappling happening over a long period of time which will allow the foundation of trust to more fully cure.

If you build upon this foundation too soon, you may risk overwhelming the burden of the trust foundation that will not withstand the test of daily wear, or worse, when the crisis of distress in the marriage arises, and the strength does not hold. The best way to avoid this is to allow time for the process so that time is now an asset and a tool in the process of recreating trust. This will be difficult for some. It will seem that a number of your gestures or actions prove your desire to trust and be trusted. However, like a precious garden in the field that requires a season of planting, nurturing, and reaping, so too will the trust in your marriage take time to mature to its full yield. It will be vital to remember this in the moments of frustration, anger, and sadness. It will seem as though your partner will never trust you again. For some it will seem that, as much as you want to trust your partner, all of your efforts to do so are futile. When this happens, remember that the trust in your marriage requires duration and as such may be in its own season of sowing, nurturance, or preparation for reaping. It may not be fully visible, but know that if you are doing the work to restore the trust in your marriage, the seeds are there.

It is during the process of duration and repetitive trust building behaviors that the seeds of trust are cultivated for growth. You can slowly begin to trust again, and you can slowly begin to garner reliance in your trust. Like any harvest that awaits its time, so too is the duration working to help grow the trust in your marriage. When frustrations arise, take time to talk to one another about the deeper primary emotions. Look for opportunities to discuss ways to affirm one another's work in fervently enduring and patiently waiting for the eventual product of your efforts to rebuild the trust in your marriage.

I explained to Kevin and Rebecca that their times together in the open water were great opportunities to practice rebuilding trust in the marriage through recreation. Piloting the boat requires teamwork, and though there may be only one person at the helm at a time, it requires the entire team to ensure that they have all they need to arrive at their destination safely. For Kevin and Rebecca, it would require relying on one another's abilities and knowing that, when needed, they had each other's backs. Although some days the proverbial relationship waters may be calm and with careful planning one could minimize the opportunities for rough waves, the reality is that sometimes the tide can still churn and catch you off guard. When it does, though, the desire to flee the storm and retreat will be tempting and understandable. However, sometimes in running for cover you can still be caught in the storm. When this happens, know that though you are in a difficult climate, it is only weather and, as such, changes. You can treat this storm as difficult, certainly, but you may also view it as essentially a different type of weather. It will require time, practice, and relentless effort to obtain the skills needed to navigate the changes to which you are unaccustomed. When you arrive at your destination, you will have obtained the hard-earned lessons from this journey and can take them on to your next one. You will be able to share in this together because without each other, it would have been impossible. It will be a story for the generations and a lasting legacy of your voyage together.

Writing Prompt

Take some time to assess the current level of trust in your relationship. Imagine that trust was a measured by temperature. If you had a thermometer, what would the temperature of trust measure on the thermometer? Imagine what the temperature was before the affair. Maybe the temperature has always read low? Maybe it was high before, and now it hardly registers on the relationship instrumentation panel? Perhaps trust measured high before the betrayal and is still hovering near the original, but it is not where you want it to be?

Review the chapter and questions above in order to reflect on your goals for improving trust within your relationship. Once you have done this, draw a pictorial representation of the status of trust within your relationship. You will do this by drawing an image of a thermometer. Get creative in your drawing. Place numbered markings within the thermometer to represent the numbered response you will give the substance filling the instrument of trust. Number the markings from 1–100. After this is complete, fill in the space with a colored writing utensil to show the amount of trust represented on your trust thermometer. You may do this activity a couple of times to demonstrate the trust thermometer reading before and after the affair. You may also do this to demonstrate the desired reading on your trust thermometer.

Once this is complete, take some time to write your responses and process with your partner where your level of trust is within the relationship. Remember that this is relationship trust and the gain in helping your partner to understand your thoughts and feelings will occur best with emphasis on explaining trust and distrust within the relationship versus within your partner. As explained in previous chapters, your relationship is an entity in which you and your partner regularly invest. The purpose here is not to blame, but rather to explain the ways in which you both experience feelings of distrust within the relationship entity for the purpose of being heard, understood and identifying measurable ways which will demonstrate goals for improvement by each partner.

CHAPTER 9

EMOTIONAL REGULATION: HOW TO MANAGE YOUR TRIGGERS

Now that we know what triggers are, it will be helpful to have ways to manage the intensely felt emotions that correlate with them.

We previously discussed the nervous system response when experiencing a looming threat. This was characterized as the fight-or-flight response to danger. What we have not discussed is what your specific triggers are that activate the protective response and what you can do to deactivate them. While this book cannot tell you what your triggers are, it can help you identify what they are through a few simple steps.

Once you identify what your triggers are, you can practice using several ways—to be discussed later in the chapter—to help regulate the moments of panic and fear when you've been triggered.

What Are Triggers?

Your triggers are cognitive cues that take you back to the felt emotional experience of a previous trauma. Your triggers can activate the memory of felt emotions, thoughts, and actions. When you are triggered, you may presently find yourself behaving in a way that mirrors the past. Your emotions may seem just as real and present as the day you experienced the trauma. Though a moment ago you may have been at rest, the occurring cognitive cue sets off an avalanche of past feelings from a moment in time that now seems like eternity. You will want to pay close attention to when familiar emotions from the day and moments you discovered the affair arise.

This applies also to the injurer, as one would not want to overlook the emotional experience of having to acknowledge the injuries to your spouse, yourself, the marriage, and ultimately your family. For the injurer, the overwhelming guilt that comes up during triggering moments may be masked by indifference or anger. Many times, for these individuals, the weight of the guilt becomes so overwhelming that it requires mechanisms to manage the burgeoning guilt and sadness in order to keep from drowning in those feelings. This is not to assume that every injurer who acts indifferently will have this experience. There may yet be some individuals who truly may not have come to terms with the repercussions of their actions and thus have not taken full responsibility for infidelity in their marriage. Assuming the partner who has committed adultery has at least begun to account for these repercussions, it would be detrimental to the affair recovery process to not acknowledge the emotional distress that both partners experience on the path to healing. With this in mind, it will be vital for couples to understand what their triggers or cues are in the environment as well as understanding what their partner's triggers are as well.

Understanding one another's triggers will help to engender compassion and awareness of the emotional challenges each of you experience in the marriage, though in different ways. In order to do this, let's explore what strategies may be taken in order to help you identify your emotional triggers.

1. *Audit Your Sensations*—Look for signs of physical or emotional discomfort throughout the day. You may not be able to identify the specific emotion you are experiencing throughout the day. This may look like a moment where your stomach begins to cramp or your heart starts to race. Maybe you are sensing your temperature rise and begin to start sweating. Perhaps you have this general feeling of fear pulsing throughout your body. Many times our body will know before our mind has had time to fully process the conditions that have contributed to our uncomfortable sensations. Knowing this gives us an advantage in being able to fully lean on our senses as thermometers to our general emotional

disposition. Observe your inner emotional state throughout the day for emotional and physical feelings of discomfort.

2. *Grab the Wheel*—Psychologist Robert Plutchik created a behavioral health tool used as a resource for improving emotional literacy. Known as the Plutchik Wheel, this tool is a circular wheel composed of core and secondary emotions. It is quite a ubiquitous tool and you may have seen them in classrooms, medical offices, and online. Locate a printable emotion wheel in a size that you can discreetly carry in your purse or pocket. Grab this wheel throughout the day when you sense discomfort or simply at periodic intervals through the day in order to best determine what your secondary and core emotions are in the moment. Just as important, once you can articulate the emotions, evaluate why they were just triggered so that you can contact a friend, journal your thoughts, communicate with your partner, or use other methods to work through the emotions.

3. *Analyze the Evidence*—Now that you have identified where the discomfort is in your mind or body and have sifted through the proverbial emotional wheel of your psyche, determine what in the environment has an association or a link to the emotional experience you are now having. What you are trying to do is determine the interaction between what is considered the physical environment and the intrapsychic environment in order to assess associations that had been created in the moment of emotional distress or trauma. It may be a smell that takes you back to the same or similar smell present when you experienced the traumatic event. It may be a sound, location, or something less concrete, like the celebration of a holiday or a day of the week. It can be anything, because these associations are specific to the individual. Therefore, it will be important to hone in on your unique experience of discomfort when emotional triggers are activated. Gathering and analyzing your emotions, physical sensations, and environmental associations will help you to better understand the precipitating factors or variables needed to activate your triggers.

Once you implement these three steps, during or after a triggering moment, it will be important to keep track of your response when seeking to down regulate the emotions. Keeping track will help you determine what are the best interventions or coping mechanisms to help you process the emotional distress and thereby return to the present moment. Managing the stress will help you separate the trauma of having discovered the affair from the present-day moments of healing in the aftermath.

The best way to do this is to experiment with several approaches in order to find what works best for you. Additionally, what works best now may not be best later. This underscores again the importance of keeping track of your triggers in order to preventatively access resources to assist you with moments of intensely felt emotions. The more implements you can have in your arsenal, the more control you will have in being able to process intensely felt emotions in a healthier way.

As with any improvement plan, some of you may not experience any relief with the implementation of these strategies. They are meant to be an addition to a broader approach in seeking help for your affair recovery. This broader approach will look different for every couple and may include a variety of tactics, which will be discussed in the next chapter. However, having some basic tools to assist you in your overall plan in seeking help for marriage will go far in managing moments of distress. Below you will find a general introduction in to the types of resources you may find useful in managing moments of distress. These are not written as an explicit guide for implementation but rather as an announcement of tools accessible with additional personal research, community, professional, or natural supports. Here are a few of these strategies:

4. *Deep Breathing*—This technique offers a variety of benefits, although for our purpose in this book, we will focus on how deep breathing helps reduce bodily distress, and thereby assists with better emotional rest and regulation. Remember that when you are breathing, the goal is to pace your breath in order to breathe deeply. Deep, paced, structured breaths are the opposite of what often happens when we are in a state of panic and fear. When we are in panic and emotional distress, we may find ourselves taking shallow, quick, and disorganized breaths. Breathing in this manner will almost certainly exacerbate or—at minimum—prolong the physical and emotional discomfort.

5. *Progressive Muscle Relaxation*—Dr. Edmunds Jacobson helped to develop an approach to calming nervous physiology in the early 1900s. He discovered that progressive muscle relaxation was a technique that could help relieve physiological distress by essentially tightening and relaxing muscles throughout the body.[33] You will want to start with one region of the body and progressively move through additional regions. For instance, you may start with your lower feet and legs and move to the upper portion of your body, ending with parts of your head and face. It will

be important to practice progressive muscle relaxation in a comfortable, stress-reducing environment. This will certainly include comfortable seating. Determine what will be a stress-reducing environment in order to engage in progressive muscle relaxation and then practice. It may be helpful to begin practicing your progressive muscle relaxation for 5-10 minutes initially. However, there may be times when you are experiencing a trigger and would prefer to utilize more time. When this happens, take the moments you do have in order to focus on isolating parts of the body where you are most likely to carry stress in order to begin tightening these muscle groups and then releasing the tension with intention.

6. *Guided Imagery*—Guided imagery (GIM) was originally created by American Music Therapist Helen Lindquist Bonny as a music-based practice.[32] In my understanding, it is a technique used where you are activating or reengaging parts of the brain with imagined stimuli. The goal of guided imagery is to use artificially engineered stimuli from our imagination in order to healthily conjure emotions and responses, which can help bring us back to a state of rest and safety. This will be important as you encounter triggers in the road to recovery from the affair in your marriage. This tool can help you to regulate intensely felt emotions during known triggers and prepare you to preventatively stabilize what may at times feel like cyclical emotions on the journey to healing. Practicing guided imagery can be used almost anywhere and at any time. It can afford you the privacy in managing negatively experienced reactions and emotions when in spaces where it may not feel safe to share what may be concerning you in the moment. It can also be used as a part of your daily regime in helping you to regularly mitigate the overwhelming emotions that may occur after the affair. Lastly, guided imagery can also be used as a co-creating space for emotional regulation on the road to recovery. As a couple, you may find that engaging in guided imagery can be a soothing activity, one where a script becomes a guide to increase emotionally co-regulated moments within the marriage. As a word of caution, some may find this exercise triggering when executed with a partner. If so, it is okay to create this space independently as well. Again, the goal is to open up opportunities where you have healthy alternatives and strategies for returning to a space of felt safety and security. If this is something that interests you, try using guided imagery whenever you feel comfortable to do so. There are a number of ways in which you may ascertain scripts, such as through books, online articles, journals, and other resources. Begin slowly and eventually find a routine where this strategy may work for you.

7. *Journaling*—Journaling is simply putting pen to paper. Of course, it may be pencil to paper, marker to paper, or craft to paper. It may vary from one person to another in terms of ways in which the journal is used, the tools or implements that are used, and the purpose for which it is used. However, there is one core thread to journaling, and that is essentially being able to document with your thoughts, behaviors, and emotions in mind. Documenting what is often unseen and unprocessed through the process of seeing what lies just beneath is the benefit to journaling. Having a tool that allows you to slowly examine and create from the heart and mind can help you to bring what is often unspoken and without words to the forefront. Here it is truly possible to communicate while not having uttered a word. This can be extremely validating when you can acknowledge what has been inadequately represented up to that point. The feelings you carry but are too afraid to speak aloud, the things you do and are still unsure of, and the thoughts you have that have yet to be fully understood are prime motivations for journaling. Journaling can be done daily, sporadically, or methodically. The key is to find ways in which this tool can work for you. Some may find journaling to be reminiscent of writing a letter, and it can be that too. In truth, journaling can be any way of documenting what is as yet unknown in order to make it known. You may practice journaling in a number of different ways. For instance, you may find that writing on college-ruled paper, in a bound journal, notebook, sketch pad, canvas, newspaper, or other forms of recording your thoughts will be a convenient and interesting tool to use in your endeavor to capture the internal. The key is to find a method that interests you, keeps you engaged, and ultimately helps to bring you some relief, validation, and understanding.

8. *Exercise*—You may find in your research that there is a vast amount of literature and research on the topic of the interconnectedness of the mind and body and what role exercise can play in our overall mental health and well-being. Exercise not only helps condition our body to take on the task of living, but living physically and emotionally well. Exercise may not necessarily solve the problems of repairing the injury in marriage; however, helping your body to develop strength, discipline, endurance, and mastery of function can translate to skillful gains in your emotional health as well. Additionally, there is significant information on the benefits of increased blood circulation generated from exercise on mood and emotional disposition. This increased blood circulation not only helps your body, but it also helps your mind. The combination of

exercise and its effects thus are synergistic in that the more you exercise and the more you experience the benefits of paced breathing, the more your capacity increases for discomfort, endurance, intentional rest, disciplined repetition, and focused connection to a goal. This can all translate to improvements in your general emotional and psychological health. Exercise is a simple resource that almost anyone can use as a preventative tool for managing difficult emotions. Though in this section we are emphasizing the psychological benefits to exercise, it is still important to consult with a physician prior to beginning any new exercise plan, as individual differences will vary greatly from person to person. The idea behind preventative intervention in your preparedness plan is to be able to have a long-acting source of relief when painful moments arise. This will balance well with your other fast-acting tools that are used during acute episodes.

9. *Rehabilitative Services*—Rehabilitation services are interventions that are used to help individuals return to a relatively equilibrized emotional, physical, or developmental state. For instance, when you have been injured in an accident, you may find yourself assigned to, for example, a physical therapist, an occupational therapist, or, depending on the accident, a speech pathologist. Others may find themselves taking an alternative approach to treatment that may include other forms of integrative medicine, such as massage therapy, acupuncture, music therapy, animal-assisted therapy, or others. Both traditional and alternative medicines provide a rich landscape where individuals may research and select a uniquely fitted approach to seek help after having experienced an emotionally traumatizing incident. The affair then becomes the backdrop in which individuals are prompted to pursue treatment in order to stabilize the resulting injuries in the wake of the emotional wounding. Therefore, obtaining treatment is no different than accepting help for any other type of wound, such as a broken leg or an arm. Now, you may not require an X-ray, speech pathologist, occupational therapist, or cast to help treat this psychic internal injury; however, though it may not be as visible as the deformation of the broken limb in our example, it is no less important to use therapeutics to help treat the affected area. It is in fact just as important as any other visible component of our being and sometimes requires rehabilitative intervention as well. This may include a range of applicable services, as noted above. Assess what your needs are currently and experiment with a few rehabilitative approaches in order to find the best support in your journey of recovery and healing.

10. *Laughter and Recreation*—This one may seem obvious, but it is frequently overlooked when we are contending with conflict and difficulty. Perhaps it is because it seems counterintuitive to find space for laughter and recreation when what seems more natural after a traumatic event is to contend with negative emotions. However, it is for this reason that you will want to add levity and activities that bring you enjoyment in order to counterbalance the inevitable stress that comes when our fight-or-flight receptors are activated after an affair is revealed. Engaging in things that interest you and help you to reset your sense of internal rest and calm will help develop strength and resilience in moments where you are most in need of those qualities. It is not that what has happened in your marriage is no less serious; it is because of how serious the matter is that you will want to balance the importance of focus in the work of repairing your marriage. You can do this through events, trips, entertainment, social gatherings, arts, comedy, music, horseback riding, dancing, games, or simply just regularly walking in order to cultivate endurance and capacity to be able to take on the task of healing and repairing your marriage over time in a healthy way.

There are more strategies that may be used in your efforts to help manage negatively experienced triggers. The goal here is to help you begin the journey in discovering what will work best for you, as these are strategies that can be used for both the injured and injurer.

The tools can be used independently, although they are best used as a comprehensive approach to help you manage intensely felt emotions. For instance, instead of thinking of deep breathing as a singular intervention, try adding deep breathing to your progressive muscle relaxation series and with your guided imagery. You may research and draft your own guided imagery script in a journal and practice regulating your emotions with your imagined ideal state of rest and sense of safety. You might also decide to schedule a massage, take up dancing, watch a funny film, revisit a favorite game, or start counseling, which we discuss more in depth in the next chapter. You may purchase additional resources that contain these and other supports as you work to define what interventions serve you best.

The most important thing to remember is that there are ways to handle negative emotions and triggers. The sense of helplessness can be a strong ingredient contributing to the overall negative cocktail of emotions and responses which arise when triggers appear in the environment. However, there are things that you can do to help begin to bring some relief from the inundation that shows up when you least expect it.

Writing Prompt:

Take a moment to determine and jot down the strategies that you currently use to manage your triggers. Next, create a list of additional ways that you may manage emotional triggers. Start with ideas that seem interesting initially and then move on to experiment with the practice strategies for emotional regulation which feel most comfortable to you. Keep a journal of your responses to both current and new ways you have tried in order to compile a list of helpful strategies to manage intensely felt emotions.

CHAPTER 10
WHEN TO SEEK PROFESSIONAL HELP

Kevin needed to answer the question he carried within himself. That question was born out of previous wounds from much earlier than the affair, but now, being much more mature and grown up, the question has increased in breadth and strength. His need to know was initially subconscious, but he had become consciously unaware of what he needed. Sometimes he would share the question aloud, but he would give it as a statement during arguments between him and Rebecca rather than a question. He would declare that what he did for his partner was never good enough for her. He declared that during arguments with her, often with tremendous bravado. However, the question was a much softer and fragile echo inside the chambers of his identity.

When the question inside his psychic corridors was asked, the answer was not quite as loud. Sometimes the response came as a deep whisper. In fact, there were moments inside himself where the response never came. At other times, the answer was there without even asking. In fact, he feared the answer more than the question. When Kevin questioned whether what he did was good enough for his wife, the answer was a resounding *no*. It was not that Rebecca ever directly uttered these words or anywhere near said them. For him, much of the proof was in the evidence he had been unwittingly collecting: there was proof in the tone she used to speak to him when discussing things for the household. There were times when she did not answer his call in the afternoon, when he was simply checking on her well-being for the day. Other times the proof was decreased receptiveness to intimacy and initiation of sex. To Kevin, the evidence was everywhere, and the verdict had been settled. In the case of Kevin vs. Kevin in the court of worth, it seemed that he would be judged not good enough. To Kevin, there was nothing Rebecca could say or do to change the outcome. All he could do was cope with the consequences.

Meanwhile, Rebecca had no idea of the degree of struggle that Kevin endured daily, as she was consumed by her own guilt and fear of abandonment. Of course, she knew that she had hurt her partner deeply, but since she made every effort to detail her accountability and fault in the matter, she assumed that Kevin would easily lay the blame on her, which would allow her to take on the brunt of the burden. She would take the brunt gladly, too. At least by carrying the blame, she would know that Kevin was still with her, connected to her. Sure, it would not be the ideal marriage, but it would be the only way that she could render any sense of security and her own evidence that he would not leave her. She told herself that as long as she could just focus on her own actions, that would alleviate her partner's fears that something like this could ever happen again.

However, what she did not account for was the growing burden that she was carrying. Sometimes it felt like everything was her fault. It was overwhelming at times. When Kevin argued that she was not picking up her calls while on a break or at work, she wanted to tell him about her day and the demands at work that were affecting her schedule and stress levels, but she rarely did, because it might trigger a reminder of the affair (since that is where the affair had begun). She feared that the affair reminder could then remind him of his unhappiness in the marriage and with her. This would inevitably lead to the desire to finally leave the marriage, it seemed to Rebecca. So, she tried her best to avoid potential reminders, since she was not fully sure of Kevin's triggers. When she had a tough day at work and felt overwhelmed and diminished, she kept it to herself and instead offered a quick apology about missing the call. When Kevin wanted to be intimate, she feared that intimacy itself would be a hotbed of negative emotional triggers and not lovemaking, which she had always enjoyed previously with her partner. It is not that she no longer desired to be with him sexually; it was that she wondered how he could possibly desire to still be with her, knowing what she had done to him. Though she longed to be close to him more now than ever before, the closer she got, the more guilt she felt and the greater the burden to carry the brunt of the responsibility for where they were in their relationship and its repair. As if constrained by some invisible magnetic field, the harder she tried to decrease the proverbial distance she knew existed in the marriage, the harder the force field seemed to repel them away from what was once a natural draw and attraction back to one another in moments of conflict.

This all came to a peak during what seemed to be one of their regularly scheduled weeknight arguments. In fact, Kevin once described these weeknight episodes of arguing as if being in one of his wife's never-ending soap opera television shows, where the characters always find some new problem to ruin what would be an otherwise happy life. Like the soap opera, you expect the outcome at the end of the show but also know there will be more drama and misfortune ahead, so stay tuned. They both anticipated the argument.

It was clear during this particular night that they could both sense the tension rising. Kevin had remarked to his wife that she took care of everyone else over him. They had just retired to their bedroom after the kids had gone to bed and were preparing for the next day. Rebecca had mentioned that she was getting up early the next day to help a volunteer organization for which she was a committee member. They had a big fundraising event coming up, one which typically required a lot of planning hours along with additional networking events to be able to meet the financial target they set for each annual goal. This year, Rebecca was tasked with more responsibility than normanl because the temporary absence of a couple other committee members. Although reluctant to take on the additional assignments, knowing that the potential time commitments could create some problems in the already-delicate position of her marriage, it pleased her to know how much she was needed in this little community she had helped to create within the organization. There, she felt like she belonged and was a part of something that saw her as an integral part of their community. Even though Rebecca knew it might cause some issues in the relationship, it was hard to pass up that feeling of belonging that she often felt when volunteering and helping others in need, although Rebecca was not fully aware of what emotional affirmation she was receiving in engaging with the volunteer organization (or others) in this way. She only knew that doing good made her feel good, and to her there was nothing wrong with that, even if it meant making some sacrifices in her personal life.

After she had mentioned that she was going to be getting up earlier to help with an upcoming fundraising event, however, Kevin told her that she was selfish and only thought about herself. Kevin shared that while she was the one who cheated, he was the one doing all the work to hold their family together. He told her that everything was on his shoulders and that while he happily assumed the leadership role for their family as provider, partner, and father, he felt that most of his efforts went unnoticed by her. Kevin shared that without his efforts, there would be no marriage, and he expressed anger that she was not also doing her part to atone for the damage she had done in their relationship. Kevin did not know that the word *atone* would be like a bullet straight through Rebecca's chest, tearing through every muscle straight to her heart. Kevin blamed Rebecca for being uncaring, cold, and unrepentant. He questioned whether he could ever forgive her and whether she was worth forgiving, for as faithful Kevin had been, it seemed to him that Rebecca had betrayed him in more ways than one. Nothing he did was good enough, nor would it ever be. For Kevin, this was a fate too much to bear any longer.

In return, Rebecca said nothing. She stood still. She couldn't move. How could she? She had been shot—not with any physical weapon, of course, but rather with words that cut through her emotional body as precisely and violently as any real weapon could physically. Rebecca panicked and started to breathe as if she were panting. She could see Kevin, but everything seemed a blur. Inside she was overwhelmed and frightened, but outside she was a statue. She was frozen.

You see, Kevin had said aloud what Rebecca had been fearing the most. He said it was all her fault and there could be no forgiveness, no redemption, and no moving forward. To Rebecca, it meant that she would be on her own again. All that she had worked hard to escape and prevent—the lack of a stable home in her childhood, the destruction of her hopes of having something different and healthy for her own family, a failure to save the marriage despite so much hard work—seemed to be happening anyway. Rebecca felt irredeemable, guilty, and, in the midst of all this, alone. To be alone was what she feared the most, and she felt it more now than ever before. As she stood there, solid in front of her partner and with tears now in her eyes, she uttered three words: "We need help."

Couples may find that seeking help will not be a linear process, nor will it look the same for every couple when pursuing outside help in the aftermath of an affair. Seeking additional help can be a varied resource in the overall approach to restoring a rupture in the relationship.

Some couples may seek help from natural resources such as friends and family. Some will seek help from organizations and groups in the community derived from various personal affiliations, such as churches, peer groups, and other sources. Still others will want to seek help from a trained professional skilled in specific strategies to assist the couple with proven methodologies that help with sensitive and/or complex matters after an affair.

There are a number of different reasons a couple may seek one route over another in their pursuit of affair recovery assistance. We will discuss a few different ways in which a couple can obtain outside assistance for help here. Note that I do not make any specific recommendations about which will be best for you, as each situation will depend on the couple and their specific needs. We will, however, discuss when it may be helpful to seek professional help for any time when or if you find yourself in need of possible clinical support.

Friends and Family—Many couples seek out natural support in their efforts to find refuge and counsel in the pain following the revelation of a marital affair. You may seek solace in sharing sensitive information with others who may know you the best. In connecting with these natural supports, you may find that you will not have to provide as many details about your situation as you would with someone who is orienting to you and your experiences for the first time. This familiar individual will come with a context in knowing who you are, what your likes and dislikes are, some understanding of the things that are causing your distress, and perhaps knowledge of the history of your relationship. This relational support may bring with it companionship, familial care, affection, charity, and connectedness. Having these aspects available to you in moments of conflict and emotional distress can be a tremendous asset to the support strategies you put in place in your affair recovery.

There may be, however, liabilities that come with inviting close family and friends into the process as well. For instance, you may find that sharing such personal information may lead to judgment that may resonate differently than the fear of judgment from a stranger where there is no personal relational investment. A stranger providing skewed feedback may not cause as much distress as that from someone who does not know and is only minimally invested in your life. Simply put, what someone who does not know you well says about you is just not as important as what someone you care for and who knows you could say. When someone who is close to you makes a comment on something that is important to you, it often carries more influence and thus has the potential to bring with it both positive and negative impacts. This dynamic therefore causes some to shy away from the possibility of risking the negative effects of openly acknowledging a marital affair with another loved one, as it opens up the potential of negative consequences felt both by the one sharing and the one about whom information is being shared. Suddenly, in sharing with those you trust and lean on for support in other matters pertaining to life, you find yourself guarding and protecting a secret among secrets in order to stave off the potential for more emotional heartache occurring within the marriage—and sometimes within yourself—because of the choices you made. For this reason, you may keep the revelation of a marital affair private from those who are closest to the relationship, or at least for a period of time, until both partners decide what will be right for them in crafting a much needed support plan in pursuit of healing a marriage.

Churches and Other Affiliated Organizations—There are times when a couple may forgo the natural support in their family and friend networks in order to seek out resources that are perhaps not as closely connected to them. In doing so, the couple is able to find support and possibly an ally to the relationship without the intimately personal relationship that often comes through the natural support found in family and friends. In seeking support through faith-based groups and other organizations that align with similar values held in the couple's approach to marriage and relationship mending, they are able to obtain help with minimal fear of judgment. In seeking this route for support, they are able to obtain community, empathy, and a sense of added privacy by partnering with an organization that purports to understand the uniqueness and sensitivity of the experience being addressed. You may find that seeking help from a resource in your community may also provide the same sense of sensitivity support without the secondary relational risks in sharing your journey with a close friend and/or family member.

This route may take several different paths. You may, for instance, find that sharing with your faith-based leader and/or a specific ministry in your place of worship will be the best place to obtain help in your affair recovery journey. In pursuing this route, you will be obtaining support from a place that emphasizes both your physical journey in recovery but also enables you to tap into a spiritual source that may add a much needed element in your overall approach to healing and marital wellness. Perhaps you will find instead that a local peer support organization that emphasizes marriage enrichment and fellowship will be the best choice in order to meet other couples who are weathering a familiar storm while simultaneously drawing from a community of support in your endeavor. The direction you take in this category of desired assistance will depend on your needs and geographic location. Of course, with technology, help has limitless boundaries, so you may find that the organizational support you seek is perhaps right at your fingertips on your computer. Whichever type of community support you select, take the time to ensure that both you and your partner will find a level of care and comfort required to gain the trust where both of you will be able to freely accept the support of a neutral organizing body.

Marriage Counseling and Other Professional Help—Many couples seek out marriage counseling in the midst of relational distress. More infrequently, couples might pursue marriage counseling as a preventative measure, but generally only when their relationship is on the brink of disruption. Therefore, it would make sense that during a period of immense emotional betrayal and emotional distress in the marriage, a couple would also consider seeking professional clinical help through marriage counseling, individual counseling for their marriage, marriage coaching, and/or group therapy support for the marriage after an affair. There are few greater emotional traumas within the relationship than that of a loved one who has committed a betrayal of trust and emotional safety. In addition, the knowledge of having helped to create an affliction within the marriage and your partner can trigger a pain and shame so overwhelming that one would be hard-pressed to come from under without the right helping hand. This is where professional help comes in. Seeking professional counseling for assistance is a specific type of support that you and your partner may desire to help you address relationship troubles as well as emerging or worsening emotional clinical symptoms that affect multiple life domains, such as career, social, and personal functioning. Essentially, when you notice that coping mechanisms seemingly used to manage the hurt subsequent to the discovery of an affair begin to negatively affect multiple areas of your life over a period of time, then it is possible that a consultation with a mental health professional, or perhaps your primary care physician, will be the next helpful step in your efforts to heal. Symptoms may look different for each individual. Therefore, instead of focusing on the their various manifestations, we will instead hone in on the idea that seeking professional help often happens when emotional responses are negatively affecting your quality of life and/or to the degree that they are negatively affecting multiple life domains. For instance, you may notice that your routine preparing for the day has changed in a way that negatively affects your ability to accomplish customary tasks. Perhaps you notice that how you would engage socially has progressively or dramatically shifted in ways that run counter to your usual personal socialization needs. Maybe you have noticed that your professional interactions and/or goals pale in comparison to your current desires and motivation to engage rituals at work and within your career. The key to recognizing that you may be in need of professional mental and/or medical help is to observe the underlying patterns in your mood, thoughts, and behaviors in order to determine the degree of how they affect your desired quality of life. Similarly, observe where the effects of managing the emotional injury from the affair, as either the injured and the injurer, negatively impact multiple facets of your personal life, creating a chasm between your present and the healthier version of life you strive to experience. When you can identify these factors as contributing elements to what may feel like a frenzied emotional space of life at work, at home, and in relationships—or for what may feel like a flat, sedate experience of life that once seemed vibrant—then you will be able to pursue appropriate forms of behavioral health that best fit your needs. You may go online to research the best type of professional support, contact a friend or associate for referral, or start with your general medical practitioner in order to obtain facilitated help in locating the best choice.

It is important to note that there is no wrong time to determine that you need additional support. The sooner you can identify that you need help, the easier it will be to identify the best route to obtain relief from your current symptoms and ultimate strategies for maintaining progress. This is important because each of us perceive and respond to traumatic events in different ways.

While there may be a general consensus on the kind of support available to those with similar needs, the implementation may look different from individual to individual. Knowing this can help you to accept the recovery process and healing time that you will specifically need in order to heal from your emotional wounds.

Once Rebecca and Kevin identified that they needed professional help, they asked a few friends if they knew of a professional marriage counselor they could recommend. They both researched my practice online and determined that they would embark upon an evidence-based process for helping couples to heal from marital trauma. In doing so, they were able to ask questions about the methodologies I use to help couples heal and transition from marital injury toward repair in their marriage. Once they felt comfortable with my responses, we began a regular course of treatment for their marriage through scheduled counseling sessions.

Mending and rebuilding the emotional wounds to the relationship was not a quick process, and though they both initially thought this endeavor would take some time, they shared that they were in some ways still surprised by how much of a time commitment it took to fully excavate the challenges within the relationship and effectively process the issues in their marriage.

However, what was most surprising for them, as they shared during our discharge session, was how possible it is to have a healthy marriage in the face of betrayal. Now they feel they can face almost any other issue together. The most impossible issue they had each thought was insurmountable to overcome now made everything else look possible by going through the process of healing. This made them more confident in their marriage and in their ability to use strategies to maintain the health of their marriage every single day.

For them, marriage was no longer about the day they had pledged their lives to one another all those years ago. It was about active creation. Marriage for them was like an organism that required nurturance and sustenance; without it, the relationship would risk either failure or, worse, become a shell of what it was meant to be. In order to realize the relationship they both envisioned, they understood that their marriage required both of them in their self-aware state to be personally invested in their process of self-improvement but also interdependent managers of the marital being—one composed of both partners, and one which necessitated a daily supply of relationship ingredients to keep the relationship alive and well.

Once they both had this revelation, they saw the relationship was no longer the relationship they had had. In fact, it was Kevin who had once used the word *atrophy* to describe the relationship and their connection in the earlier stages of marriage work. What they had both discovered was that in doing the work to repair their marriage, the old, earlier parts of their relationship had ceased, and what had emerged was a different but deeply gratifying relationship underneath. This time they would give the relationship what it needed to survive now that they knew what its requirements are.

Equipped with this knowledge, they determined that this new marital life would be best acknowledged with new vows for this emerging relationship with a commitment to demonstrate to one another that, from this point forward, "every day, I do."

Writing Prompt

Take a moment to determine and jot down what additional supports you and your partner may benefit from in the marriage. You may desire to start with writing your thoughts on the benefits and consequences of each resource and discuss with your partner what will be best for your marriage.

CHAPTER 11

REWRITING YOUR VOWS

If you are reading this and have reached the end of the book, you may be wondering at this point how the story ended with Rebecca and Kevin. I could tell you that all of their challenges were resolved and that they lived happily ever after. In saying such, you would see right through the fantasy of such an outcome. However, the reality is that many couples who have walked the path from relational betrayal toward recovery have an expectation that simply beginning the road to repair will suffice for marital reconciliation.

The truth is that expectations are best expressed, and almost certainly better shared, with your partner in marriage. An example of this may simply be your desires expressed through word or deed. It may arise in passing conversation, an intimate discussion between you and your partner, a written note detailing your needs, or in other ways.

Your vows are just another example of expectations set for yourself, your partner, and within the marriage.

While it may be tempting to establish your vows as the preeminent authority for the relationship construct, as if they had been canonized where no other approving principles in the marriage could be accepted, it may hinder the growth capacity for this working agreement. From this standpoint, your vows risk being viewed as a memorial to your wedding day, intended only for celebratory rituals and only as an afterthought to the more prominent needs of the day.

On the contrary, your vows should be seen not only as the declarative articles from which your marriage is drawn, but also as a working body of principles in which you both forever settle and from which you both perpetually create as the needs and expectations of the marriage change. In this perspective, your marital promises and expectations are preeminent, but they are also changeable, and that is because the relationship will inevitably go through changes. It will evolve and hopefully mature. In doing so, you and your partner have the unique opportunity to regularly remember so that you can readily seize the daily opportunities that each of you have to acknowledge the oaths you made to one another in ways that reflect your marriage today.

The good news is that you will not need to start from scratch. You can add to your vows, reassemble, or rewrite your vows. The choice is for you and your partner. Remember that the goal is to more thoroughly express and realize your relationship expectations for your marriage. This will require conversation and quite possibly ample time to qualify these expectations and promises.

As in the *work* analogy discussed earlier in the book, your marriage requires work, and with any form of work, the regular duties assigned within should reflect the position you occupy and the larger strategic goal. In this view, your role as a partner and the daily performance of such in the marriage should also reflect the larger goal or, better said, the vows made within your marriage.

Kevin and Rebecca realized this, and when they began to see the changes in their marriage and hope for their future, they wanted to revisit their vows, seeking to capitalize on the opportunity to capture the renewal of their marriage. They realized that there would be other challenges ahead, and that even though life as happily ever after was an invitation to false imaginations, their story was instead one of challenge, transformation, and hope that, in all of these things, they could face almost anything ahead if they did so together.

Following is an excerpt of Rebecca and Kevin's rewritten vows. Instead of focusing on what they included, instead pay attention to the ways in which their promises were made. Doing so will help you and your partner to consider what a copy of your very own would look like. After the excerpt, you will find a template in order to assist you both with shaping, reassembling, or adjusting your new vows so that you can direct them toward your own steps to repair and heal your marriage daily.

Rebecca

Kevin:

To me, you are a safe place when I feel scared; you comfort me with your presence and your words.

When I am alone, you stand next to me, and when it's hard to be seen, you give me room so that I am free to be myself.

I feel celebrated when you greet me after a long day and missed when you send me off into the world. It's not loud, but it speaks volumes to me and shows me how much I am cherished by you. I remember the time you held my hand when my grandmother passed. You knew how close I was to her and how I had loved spending time with her since I was a child; you never grew weary of my shield because you saw through to the deep sadness I was carrying in trying to be strong for everyone else. I took strength from your hands.

Your words bring me peace any time there is trouble on the horizon. They are like the thunder in a storm, not to bring fear but to bring attention to your presence and your protection while in the storm; our family is secure with you.

I vow to bring you closer to me when I am afraid of being vulnerable and to not push you away.

Instead of shutting down, I will open up and hold nothing back.

As your friend, I vow to be there for you as you are and have always been with me.

I vow to tell you the truth even when the risks seem too great.

I vow to listen to you and tell you that I understand only when I do because I strive to know you more and more. You are the most exciting mystery.

And I vow to spend the rest of my life learning and getting to explore you.

I vow to never stop improving as a partner so that I can get better at loving you every day, because I vow to honor our marriage as worthy of the daily work I do for us—always.

Kevin

Rebecca:

The first time I saw you, I knew you were the one. I knew it then, and I still know it now.

Your smile makes me feel like the strongest man alive, and I'm ready to conquer the world for our family.

I remember the times we would stay up for hours discussing our dreams and plans for the future. You knew even then how to make me comfortable opening up about things I had never even shared before. You are my confidant.

Your encouragement is the reason I started the business. You knew that I needed that extra support. When I doubt myself, you are right there to remind me of who I know I am.

You make our house a home for all of our children. Though our family is blended, we are all connected together. You do that with the way you care for us.

Your unyielding faith and hope in every challenge inspires me to be a better man by God's grace. I thank Him for sending you.

I vow to listen more deeply when your voice becomes still because I value what you say.

When you share your feelings, I vow to be vulnerable with mine.

I vow to tell you or show you daily that we are in this together. You are never alone.

I vow to hug you and remind you of how beautiful you are to me, and it is from your heart that your beauty begins.

I know no other woman like you, and I am a man for no other. You are the find to a lifetime of searching, and I vow to spend my life keeping you safe and protecting our marriage today for the rest of our lives.

APPENDIX

Marriage Vow Template

Fill in the template sentences and assemble the phrasing into a message meant for you and your partner.

You are to me _____ when you _____.

When you _____, I feel _____.

Your _____ is like _____.

I remember the time you _____ and it made me feel _____.

I believe that you are _____ and I am _____ with you.

I appreciate that you _____.

I love that you _____, and it does _____.

The best part of our love is that _____.

I can be _____ when I am with you _____.

I vow to _____ when you _____.

I promise to _____ as you _____.

I vow to _____ as we _____.

I take your _____ to be _____.

I devote my _____ to you in _____.

I pledge that I will _____.

NOTES

1. Gottman, John, and Julie Gottman, "Treating Affairs and Trauma," (course material, The Gottman Institute), https://www.gottman.com/product/treating-affairs-and-trauma/

2. "Trauma," in *Merriam-Webster.com* (Merriam-Webster, 2023). https://www.merriam-webster.com/dictionary/trauma

3. Guarino, K., and E. Chagnon, "Understanding Trauma and its Impact" in Trauma-Sensitive Schools Training Package, (Washington, DC: National Center on Safe Supportive Learning Environments, 2018). https://safesupportivelearning.ed.gov/sites/default/files/TSS_Understanding_Slides.pptx

4. Logan, Angela R., "Recognizing and Overcoming Unconscious Bias" (course material, University of Notre Dame, September 24, 2020). https://exchange.mendoza.nd.edu/media/1266/unconscious-bias-workshop_logan_9-24-2020.pptx

5. Deb Dana and Stephen W. Porges, *The Polyvagal Theory in Therapy: Engaging the Rhythm of Regulation,* (New York: W.W. Norton & Company, 2018).

6. Ibid.

7. "Understanding the Stress Response," Harvard Health, July 6, 2020, https://www.health.harvard.edu/staying-healthy/understanding-the-stress-response.

8. Ibid.

9. "Stress Effects on the Body." American Psychological Association website, November 1, 2018. https://www.apa.org/topics/stress/body

10. Ibid.

11. "Understanding the Stress Response."

12. Jude Cassidy, "The Nature of the Child's Ties," in *Handbook of Attachment: Theory, Research, and Clinical Applications*, ed. Jude Cassidy and Phillip R. Shaver, Third Edition (New York: The Guilford Press, 2016), 4.

13. Ibid.

14. Ibid.

15. Ibid., 29

16. Judith A. Feeney, "Adult Romantic Attachment: Developments in the Study of Couple Relationships," in *Handbook of Attachment: Theory, Research, and Clinical Applications,* ed. Jude Cassidy and Phillip R. Shaver, Third edition (New York: The Guilford Press, 2016), 436.

17. Cindy Hazan and Phillip Shaver, "Romantic Love Conceptualized as an Attachment Process," *Journal of Personality and Social Psychology* (1987): 52,3

18. Kim Bartholomew and Leonard Horowitz, "Attachment Styles Among Young Adults: A Test of a Four-Category Model," *Journal of Personality and Social Psychology*, (1991):61,2

19. Ibid., 220

20. "What Is Imago?" Harville & Helen, https://harvilleandhelen.com/initiatives/what-is-imago/.

21. Ibid.

22. Ibid.

23. Hendrix, Harville, *Getting the Love You Want: A Guide for Couples*, Second edition (St. Martin's Press, 2007).

24. "Primary Emotion," in *APA Dictionary of Psychology* (American Psychological Association). https://dictionary.apa.org/primary-emotion.

25. "Empathy." in *Merriam-Webster.com* (Merriam-Webster, 2023). https://www.merriam-webster.com/dictionary/empathy.

26. Cassidy, "The Nature of the Child's Ties," 8.

27. Johnson, Sue, "The New Frontier of Sex & Intimacy," TEDx University of Ottowa, July 28, 2015, video, 14:47, https://www.youtube.com/watch?v=hiVijMLH2-k.

28. Robert C. Solomon and Fernando Flores, *Building Trust: In Business, Politics, Relationships, and Life* (Oxford: Oxford University Press, 2003), 58.

29. Ibid., 89.

30. Ibid., 7.

31. "Guided Imagery and Music," in *Britannica*, accessed February 22, 2023, https://www.britannica.com/science/guided-imagery.

32. Shilagh A. Mirgain and Janice Singles, "Progressive Muscle Relaxation," VA.gov, January 25, 2021, https://www.va.gov/wholehealthlibrary/tools/progressive-muscle-relaxation.asp.

33. Solomon and Flores, *Building Trust*.

ABOUT THE AUTHOR

Angel Myers is a Licensed Marriage and Family Therapist. She is the owner of a marriage counseling practice named Angel Marriage & Family Services, where she has helped countless couples dealing with the trauma of affair recovery. She is a part-time writer on her website and social media, where you can find her at www.angelmarriageandfamily.com. When she's not writing or counseling couples, you can find her dancing the night away to Latin music and doing so as a mom of two of the most beloved teenagers.

EVERY DAY, I DO:
JOURNALING THROUGH BETRAYAL

To Vivian and Uriah, with all my love…

INTRODUCTION

Welcome to the journaling through your affair recovery workbook. This is an accompaniment to the book, "Every day, I Do: How to Rewrite your Vows After an Affair" where couples begin to explore the aftermath of an affair. This journal is intended to give readers a space to further reflect on their journey of healing through the affair recovery process. Though intended as an accompaniment, this book can also stand alone as a resource for further individual reflection and personal assessment no matter where you are in your journey of healing.

In this journal workbook, you will receive a prompt for each week. With each prompt, you will find four other sub-category questions intended to cultivate deeper insight. The sub-category questions will remain the same for each prompt and the prompt will change with each week to give you time to process and better understand where you are in your journey to healing and where you desire to go. This will happen with slow consideration of your experience during this time in your life. Therefore, do not rush through the pages. Each page brings just enough opportunity for cognitive and emotional distillation each week.

Near the end of the journal workbook, you will find two final prompts which seek to consolidate a year's worth of journaling toward healing and increased understanding. This prompt will take more time than all the others as you will be writing a letter to the version of you starting this journey one year ago. When you arrive at this marker, take time to consolidate the lessons you've gathered within yourself along the way. Though at this juncture you will be nearing the end of the journal the journey may continue.

At the end of the workbook, you will find a few resources which may assist you with your continued support. These resources are not recommendations but rather optional supports that you mind find helpful as you progress through the final phase of completion.

Additionally, if during the process of working through this workbook journal or near the completion you find that there is content that may trigger negative emotional responses, you may decide to pause your progress through the material. If this happens, feel free to discontinue the use of this journal and turn to the Appendix Section to review the list of possible resources available for further assistance. Therefore, It is important to remain attuned to your needs during moments of reflection and writing to know when to pause and refer to these and other resources where appropriate.

SELF NURTURANCE:

How do you nourish yourself? It I important to find ways to sow within your emotional psyche positive emotional encouragement as this can be like emotional food yielding fruits of strength during sensitive moments. Continue to find ways to feed your emotional self with words, actions, and thoughts which help to grow your stamina to succeed in the positive goals you have identified for yourself.

In this section, you will find 10 journal prompts that will assist you with discovering ways to cultivate healthy emotional nurturance while practicing it in your moments of quiet inquiry and reflection. Afterward, write your response to each question, each day. There are no right or wrong responses, just your truth.

1. **What are the parts of my personality I must celebrate?**

_____
_____
_____
_____

   a. How do I feel about this question ?

_____
_____

b. What do I think about seeing my answer before my eyes?

_____
_____

c. What was the first thought that came to my mind?

_____
_____

d. What do I hope as I read my response aloud?

_____
_____

2. The quality I respect most about myself?

_____
_____
_____

a. How do I feel about this question?

_____
_____

b. What do I think about seeing my answer before my eyes?

_____
_____

c. What was the first thought that came to my mind?

_____
_____

d. What do I hope as I read my response aloud?

_____

_____

3 I know that I am a valuable person because ?

_____

_____

_____

_____

a. How do I feel about this question ?

_____

_____

b. What do I think about seeing my answer before my eyes ?

_____

_____

c. What was the first thought that came to my mind ?

_____

_____

d. What do I hope as I read my response aloud?

_____

_____

4 **I tend to cherish this part of me ?**

_____
_____
_____
_____

a. How do I feel about this question ?

_____
_____

b. What do I think about seeing my answer before my eyes ?

_____
_____

c. What was the first thought that came to my mind ?

_____
_____

d. What do I hope as I read my response aloud?

_____
_____

5 **I have grown the most in this area ?**

_____
_____
_____
_____

a. How do I feel about this question ?

_____
_____

b. What do I think about seeing my answer before my eyes ?

_____
_____

c. What was the first thought that came to my mind ?

_____
_____

d. What do I hope as I read my response aloud?

_____
_____

6. You can see my creativity when I ?

_____
_____
_____
_____

a. How do I feel about this question ?

_____
_____

b. What do I think about seeing my answer before my eyes ?

_____
_____

c. What was the first thought that came to my mind ?

_____
_____

d. What do I hope as I read my response aloud?

_____
_____

7 I know there is good in me when I think about?

_____
_____
_____
_____

a. How do I feel about this question ?

_____
_____

b. What do I think about seeing my answer before my eyes ?

_____
_____

c. What was the first thought that came to my mind ?

_____
_____

d. What do I hope as I read my response aloud?

_____
_____

8   **I respect my opinion in determining ?**

_____
_____
_____

a. How do I feel about this question ?

_____
_____

b. What do I think about seeing my answer before my eyes ?

_____
_____

c. What was the first thought that came to my mind ?

_____
_____

d. What do I hope as I read my response aloud?

_____
_____

9   **I admire this about myself ?**

_____
_____
_____
_____

a. How do I feel about this question ?

_____

_____

b. What do I think about seeing my answer before my eyes ?

_____

_____

c. What was the first thought that came to my mind ?

_____

_____

d. What do I hope as I read my response aloud?

_____

_____

10. I believe in myself because ?

_____

_____

_____

_____

a. How do I feel about this question ?

_____

_____

b. What do I think about seeing my answer before my eyes ?

_____

_____

c. What was the first thought that came to my mind ?

_____

_____

d. What do I hope as I read my response aloud?

_____

_____

PRIVATE WINS

How do you recognize your accomplishments?

Sometimes we can do things that bring us the most pride even when no one may be there to acknowledge them. This however does not diminish the prize of success in proving our efforts towards a goal that we have hard fought and won. These are called *Private Wins* and they deserve our attention nonetheless.

In this section, you will find 10 journal prompts that will assist you with discovering ways to acknowledge your *Private Wins* and successes while practicing them in your moments of quiet inquiry and reflection. Afterward, write your response to each question, each day. There are no right or wrong responses, just your truth.

The time someone needed me I was there too?

_____

_____

_____

_____

a. How do I feel about this question ?

_____

_____

b. What do I think about seeing my answer before my eyes ?

_____
_____

c. What was the first thought that came to my mind ?

_____
_____

d. What do I hope as I read my response aloud?

_____
_____

2. I know I make a positive difference when I ?

_____
_____
_____

a. How do I feel about this question ?

_____
_____

b. What do I think about seeing my answer before my eyes ?

_____
_____

c. What was the first thought that came to my mind ?

_____
_____

d. What do I hope as I read my response aloud?

_____
_____

3. The goal I am most proud of ?

_____
_____
_____

a. How do I feel about this question ?

_____
_____

b. What do I think about seeing my answer before my eyes ?

_____
_____

c. What was the first thought that came to my mind ?

_____
_____

d. What do I hope as I read my response aloud?

_____
_____

4. **My kindness comes through each time I ?**

_____
_____
_____

a. How do I feel about this question ?

_____
_____

b. What do I think about seeing my answer before my eyes ?

_____
_____

c. What was the first thought that came to my mind ?

_____
_____

d. What do I hope as I read my response aloud?

_____
_____

5. **I am most proud of my ?**

_____
_____
_____
_____

a. How do I feel about this question ?

_____
_____

b. What do I think about seeing my answer before my eyes ?

_____
_____

c. What was the first thought that came to my mind ?

_____
_____

d. What do I hope as I read my response aloud?

_____
_____

6   I know I am successful at ?

_____
_____
_____
_____

a. How do I feel about this question ?

_____
_____

b. What do I think about seeing my answer before my eyes ?

_____
_____

c. What was the first thought that came to my mind ?

d. What do I hope as I read my response aloud?

7. Everyone knows that I'm good at ?

a. How do I feel about this question ?

b. What do I think about seeing my answer before my eyes ?

c. What was the first thought that came to my mind ?

d. What do I hope as I read my response aloud?

8. **I thought I would never finish but then I finally finished the ?** ♦

_____
_____
_____

   a. How do I feel about this question ?

   _____
   _____

   b. What do I think about seeing my answer before my eyes ?

   _____
   _____

   c. What was the first thought that came to my mind ?

   _____
   _____

   d. What do I hope as I read my response aloud?

   _____
   _____

9. **Today I am better than yesterday because I ?** ♦

_____
_____
_____
_____

a. How do I feel about this question ?

b. What do I think about seeing my answer before my eyes ?

c. What was the first thought that came to my mind ?

d. What do I hope as I read my response aloud?

10 I am known to be the best at?

a. How do I feel about this question ?

b. What do I think about seeing my answer before my eyes ?

c. What was the first thought that came to my mind?

_____

_____

d. What do I hope as I read my response aloud?

_____

_____

DREAMS

Even in challenging times, our heart still holds hope for our dreams both spoken and unspoken. At times, they will seem far away but you will only need to go within yourself to find that your dreams are alive and only at rest until the right time. Take a moment to reflect on your dreams. Search deep within your heart to determine what you envision for yourself. If you find that your dreams have changed, then make new ones. Be indulgent and allow yourself to dream big.

In this section, you will find 10 journal prompts that will assist you with discovering ways to discover and acknowledge your *Dreams*. Afterward, write your response to each question, each day. There are no right or wrong responses, just your truth.

1   **I hope someday that I can ?**

_____
_____
_____

   a. How do I feel about this question ?

_____
_____

b. What do I think about seeing my answer before my eyes ?

_____
_____

c. What was the first thought that came to my mind ?

_____
_____

d. What do I hope as I read my response aloud?

_____
_____

2) I have never been able but I would love to ?

_____
_____
_____
_____

a. How do I feel about this question ?

_____
_____

b. What do I think about seeing my answer before my eyes ?

_____
_____

c. What was the first thought that came to my mind ?

_____
_____

d. What do I hope as I read my response aloud?

3 I have always wanted to be ?

a. How do I feel about this question ?

b. What do I think about seeing my answer before my eyes ?

c. What was the first thought that came to my mind ?

d. What do I hope as I read my response aloud?

4. **I have never given up hope that I will ?**

_____
_____
_____

   a. How do I feel about this question ?

   _____
   _____

   b. What do I think about seeing my answer before my eyes ?

   _____
   _____

   c. What was the first thought that came to my mind ?

   _____
   _____

   d. What do I hope as I read my response aloud?

   _____
   _____

5. **It brings me joy to imagine that someday ?**

_____
_____
_____
_____

a. How do I feel about this question ?

_____
_____

b. What do I think about seeing my answer before my eyes ?

_____
_____

c. What was the first thought that came to my mind ?

_____
_____

d. What do I hope as I read my response aloud?

_____
_____

6 I imagine feeling stronger when I am?

_____
_____
_____
_____

a. How do I feel about this question ?

_____
_____

b. What do I think about seeing my answer before my eyes ?

_____
_____

c. What was the first thought that came to my mind ?

_____
_____

d. What do I hope as I read my response aloud?

_____
_____

7. The one place I've always wanted to visit ?

_____
_____
_____

a. How do I feel about this question ?

_____
_____

b. What do I think about seeing my answer before my eyes ?

_____
_____

c. What was the first thought that came to my mind ?

_____
_____

d. What do I hope as I read my response aloud?

_____
_____

8   If I could choose a different career it would be ?

_____
_____
_____

a. How do I feel about this question ?

_____
_____

b. What do I think about seeing my answer before my eyes ?

_____
_____

c. What was the first thought that came to my mind ?

_____
_____

d. What do I hope as I read my response aloud?

_____
_____

9   I smile when I think about ?

_____
_____
_____
_____

a. How do I feel about this question ?

_____
_____

b. What do I think about seeing my answer before my eyes ?

_____
_____

c. What was the first thought that came to my mind ?

_____
_____

d. What do I hope as I read my response aloud?

_____
_____

10 I always wanted to learn how to ?

_____
_____
_____
_____

a. How do I feel about this question ?

_____
_____

b. What do I think about seeing my answer before my eyes ?

_____
_____

c. What was the first thought that came to my mind?

_____

_____

d. What do I hope as I read my response aloud?

_____

_____

HOW DO I FEEL

What do you feel?

While it may be hard to answer that question right now. It is an important question to keep close as it may give you the clues needed for determining the direction in your journey, answers to moments of discomfort, and challenging thoughts that provide a disservice to your desires. Staying in touch with what you feel can help you find the answers to these questions and more.

In this section, you will find 10 journal prompts that will assist you with discovering ways to unlock and uncover emotions to answer the question *How Do I Feel?*

Reflect on your emotional words. Be specific in locating the emotion word that matches your feelings. Afterward, write your response to each question, each day. There are no right or wrong responses, just your truth.

1. **The place on my body where I carry the most tension is?**

_____
_____
_____

a. How do I feel about this question ?

_____
_____

b. What do I think about seeing my answer before my eyes?

c. What was the first thought that came to my mind?

d. What do I hope as I read my response aloud?

2. It is hard for me to express my feelings for?

a. How do I feel about this question?

b. What do I think about seeing my answer before my eyes?

c. What was the first thought that came to my mind?

d. What do I hope as I read my response aloud?

_____
_____

3   The emotion that scares me the most is?

_____
_____
_____

a. How do I feel about this question ?

_____
_____

b. What do I think about seeing my answer before my eyes ?

_____
_____

c. What was the first thought that came to my mind ?

_____
_____

d. What do I hope as I read my response aloud?

_____
_____

4. **I feel joy when?**

a. How do I feel about this question?

b. What do I think about seeing my answer before my eyes?

c. What was the first thought that came to my mind?

d. What do I hope as I read my response aloud?

5. **I have hope that what day I can feel?**

a. How do I feel about this question ?

_____
_____

b. What do I think about seeing my answer before my eyes ?

_____
_____

c. What was the first thought that came to my mind ?

_____
_____

d. What do I hope as I read my response aloud?

_____
_____

6. There is a memory that I go to when I need to feel?

_____
_____
_____

a. How do I feel about this question ?

_____
_____

b. What do I think about seeing my answer before my eyes ?

_____
_____

c. What was the first thought that came to my mind?

d. What do I hope as I read my response aloud?

7. The things I feel confident in are?

a. How do I feel about this question?

b. What do I think about seeing my answer before my eyes?

c. What was the first thought that came to my mind?

d. What do I hope as I read my response aloud?

8. **I have a healthy emotional release when I can?**

_____
_____
_____

a. How do I feel about this question ?

_____
_____

b. What do I think about seeing my answer before my eyes ?

_____
_____

c. What was the first thought that came to my mind ?

_____
_____

d. What do I hope as I read my response aloud?

_____
_____

9. **I feel soothed emotionally when I can.**

_____
_____
_____

a. How do I feel about this question?

_____
_____

b. What do I think about seeing my answer before my eyes?

_____
_____

c. What was the first thought that came to my mind?

_____
_____

d. What do I hope as I read my response aloud?

_____
_____

10 I know that I am negatively triggered when I feel?

_____
_____
_____

a. How do I feel about this question?

_____
_____

b. What do I think about seeing my answer before my eyes?

_____
_____

c. What was the first thought that came to my mind?

_____

_____

d. What do I hope as I read my response aloud?

_____

_____

STAY IN FAITH

It can be helpful to have a higher power you are cognizant of during this journey of healing and recovery. Whether it is one religion or another is for you to decide. Having this spiritual framework and *Staying in Faith* can help bring endurance when weary and in need of peace during moments of distress. Your faith in this higher power is a personal decision and is guided by your pursuit.

In this section, you will find 10 journal prompts that will assist you with discovering ways to pursue and remain in your faith during times of difficulty and challenge. Reflect on your experience with a higher power and what it means to *Stay in Faith*. Take time to reflect on your spirituality and allow these following prompts to deepen your spiritual journey. Afterward, write your response to each question, each day. There are no right or wrong responses, just your truth.

1   **I feel centered when I ?**

___

___

___

     a. How do I feel about this question ?

___

___

b. What do I think about seeing my answer before my eyes ?

_____
_____

c. What was the first thought that came to my mind ?

_____
_____

d. What do I hope as I read my response aloud?

_____
_____

2. I believe in ?

_____
_____
_____

a. How do I feel about this question ?

_____
_____

b. What do I think about seeing my answer before my eyes ?

_____
_____

c. What was the first thought that came to my mind ?

_____
_____

d. What do I hope as I read my response aloud?

3. My place of comfort is ?

a. How do I feel about this question ?

b. What do I think about seeing my answer before my eyes ?

c. What was the first thought that came to my mind ?

d. What do I hope as I read my response aloud?

4. **My values tell me that?**

_____
_____
_____
_____

   a. How do I feel about this question ?

   _____
   _____

   b. What do I think about seeing my answer before my eyes ?

   _____
   _____

   c. What was the first thought that came to my mind ?

   _____
   _____

   d. What do I hope as I read my response aloud?

   _____
   _____

5. **During times of diversity, my hope is in the fact that**

_____
_____
_____
_____

a. How do I feel about this question?

_____

_____

b. What do I think about seeing my answer before my eyes?

_____

_____

c. What was the first thought that came to my mind?

_____

_____

d. What do I hope as I read my response aloud?

_____

_____

6 I feel uplifted when I envision?

_____

_____

_____

_____

a. How do I feel about this question?

_____

_____

b. What do I think about seeing my answer before my eyes?

_____

_____

c. What was the first thought that came to my mind ?

_____
_____

d. What do I hope as I read my response aloud?

_____
_____

7. Rituals for my inner self include?

_____
_____
_____
_____

a. How do I feel about this question ?

_____
_____

b. What do I think about seeing my answer before my eyes ?

_____
_____

c. What was the first thought that came to my mind ?

_____
_____

d. What do I hope as I read my response aloud?

_____
_____

8   **My hope is in the belief that?**

_____
_____
_____
_____

   a. How do I feel about this question ?

   _____
   _____

   b. What do I think about seeing my answer before my eyes ?

   _____
   _____

   c. What was the first thought that came to my mind ?

   _____
   _____

   d. What do I hope as I read my response aloud?

   _____
   _____

9   **The meaning of life is that?**

_____
_____
_____
_____

a. How do I feel about this question ?

_____
_____

b. What do I think about seeing my answer before my eyes ?

_____
_____

c. What was the first thought that came to my mind ?

_____
_____

d. What do I hope as I read my response aloud?

_____
_____

10 I feel honored in life to be able to ?

_____
_____
_____
_____

a. How do I feel about this question ?

_____
_____

b. What do I think about seeing my answer before my eyes ?

_____
_____

c. What was the first thought that came to my mind?

_____

_____

d. What do I hope as I read my response aloud?

_____

_____

TIME CAPSULE TO MY YOUNGER SELF

Week 51: Take some time to remember this past year. How would you summarize this year? What do you see when you look back? What do you remember hearing? What smells come back to you? What dates stand out for you? What emotions return? What thoughts were constantly on repeat? Whom did you tell about your journey along the way? Who were your supporters? Where did you find help? When did you start to notice positive changes in your recovery journey?

Use the section below to jot down your initial thoughts and responses. This should be a free-flow writing moment to empty and eventually organize your thoughts for what will be the letter to yourself. The writing portion is located below. Again, there are no right or wrong answers, simply what remains true for you.

_____

_____

_____

_____

_____

_____

_____

Week 52: Below you will find a section where you can record your thoughts and response to the above journal prompts concerning this past year of affair recovery. The prompts above are suggestions and are not meant to capture this past year in totality. Therefore, take the liberty of asking yourself additional questions which will help answer this much larger question surrounding this past year's healing endeavor.

Ask, *What encouragement would I tell myself from one year ago?*

_____
_____
_____
_____
_____
_____
_____

APPENDIX

When to Seek Professional Help

Seeking professional counseling for assistance may be a specific type of support that you and your partner desire in addressing relationship concerns about adjustments occurring within marriage as well as emerging or worsening emotional clinical symptoms that affect multiple life domains such as career, social and personal functioning. Essentially, when you notice that helpful coping mechanisms previously used to manage distress after the discovery of an affair begin to wane in their effectiveness then a consultation with a mental health professional or perhaps your primary care physician may be the next helpful step in your efforts to heal. Symptoms may look different for each individual and therefore instead of focusing on the various manifestations of these, we will instead hone in on the idea that seeking professional help often happens when emotional responses are negatively affecting your quality of life and/or the degree to which they are negatively affecting multiple life domains

There are several types of providers one may seek to pursue in obtaining professional help. These are but not fully inclusive:

1. Psychiatrist
2. Licenses Therapist
3. Peer Mentoring
4. Consultation
5. Psychologist
6. Group Therapy

7. Pastoral Counseling

There are other types of helping professionals who may offer an alternative approach to help during this stage of healing. These may include for instance rehabilitation providers such as massage therapists, acupuncturists, animal therapy, recreation therapists, etc. Research, consult with your physician, and find the approach which works best for you during this time.

NOTES

Made in the USA
Las Vegas, NV
23 August 2024

94309945R00095